Best Practices in
PARISH STEWARDSHIP

Best Practices in
PARISH STEWARDSHIP

CHARLES E. ZECH

VILLANOVA UNIVERSITY
CENTER FOR THE STUDY OF CHURCH MANAGEMENT

Our Sunday Visitor Publishing Division
Our Sunday Visitor, Inc.
Huntington, Indiana 46750

The Scripture citations used in this work are taken from the *Catholic Edition of the Revised Standard Version of the Bible* (RSV), copyright © 1965 and 1966 by the Division of Christian Education of the National Council of the Churches of Christ in the United States of America. Used by permission. All rights reserved.

Every reasonable effort has been made to determine copyright holders of excerpted materials and to secure permissions as needed. If any copyrighted materials have been inadvertently used in this work without proper credit being given in one form or another, please notify Our Sunday Visitor in writing so that future printings of this work may be corrected accordingly.

Copyright © 2008, 2016 by Our Sunday Visitor Publishing Division, Our Sunday Visitor, Inc. Published 2016

21 20 19 18   3 4 5 6 7 8

All rights reserved. With the exception of short excerpts for critical reviews, no part of this work may be reproduced or transmitted in any form or by any means whatsoever without permission in writing from the publisher. Write:

Our Sunday Visitor Publishing Division
Our Sunday Visitor, Inc.
200 Noll Plaza
Huntington, IN 46750

ISBN: 978-1-68192-062-7 (Inventory No. T1805)

LCCN: 2008931957

Cover design by Rebecca J. Heaston
Interior design by Sherri L. Hoffman

PRINTED IN THE UNITED STATES OF AMERICA

CONTENTS

CHAPTER ONE — **Introduction**	9
The Meaning of Stewardship	10
The Plan of This Book	14
References	17
CHAPTER TWO — **Previous Studies**	19
Qualitative Studies	19
Patrick McNamara	19
Paul Wilkes	21
Justin Clements	23
Quantitative Studies	25
Stewardship Measures	28
A Word about Statistics	31
References	33
CHAPTER THREE — **Parish Demographic and Socioeconomic Characteristics**	35
General Characteristics	37
Age Profile	38
Life-Cycle Theory	38
Generational-Cohort Theory	39
Socioeconomic Characteristics	41
Ethnicity	43
Summary	43
References	44

CHAPTER FOUR — The Role of the Stewardship Council   45
    Membership   46
    Survey Findings   48
    Summary   51
    References   52

CHAPTER FIVE — Lay Witnesses   53
    Who Should Serve as a Lay Witness?   55
    When Should Lay Witness Talks Occur?   57
    Summary   58
    References   59

CHAPTER SIX — Other Parish Stewardship Activities   61
    Homilies   61
    Ministry Fairs and Commitment Sunday   64
    Support of Time and Talent   66
        Gift Discernment   66
        Ministry Commissioning   68
        Ministry Appreciation Dinner   68
    Parish Planning   69
    Summary   70
    References   71

CHAPTER SEVEN — Parish Formation and Education Programs   73
    Youth Programs   74
    Adult Programs   77
    Summary   79
    References   80

CHAPTER EIGHT — Parish Teachings on Parishioners' Level of Support Decisions   81
    Tithing   81
    Pledging   84
    Survey Findings   86

Summary	88
Reference	89
CHAPTER NINE — Parish Welcoming and Community-Building Activities	**91**
Welcoming Activities	96
Community-Building Activities	97
Summary	98
References	98
CHAPTER TEN — Communications on Stewardship	**101**
Communications to Focus Attention on Stewardship	102
Communications to Spotlight Contributions of Time and Talent	105
Summary	107
Reference	108
CHAPTER ELEVEN — Financial Accountability and Transparency	**109**
Stewardship in the Parish House	109
Approaches to Financial Accountability and Transparency	114
Summary	117
References	118
CHAPTER TWELVE — Eight Things That Parishes Can Do to Advance Stewardship	**119**
Best Practices in Parish Stewardship	120
Summary	124

Chapter One

INTRODUCTION

Most Catholics are surprised to learn that, compared to their Protestant friends, they rank very low in terms of their support for their Church. Beginning with Fr. Andrew Greeley's path-breaking 1987 study of Catholic financial giving, nearly every study of the topic has found that, on a percentage of income basis, Catholics contribute only about half as much to their Church as do Protestants. Most studies reveal that the typical Protestant household contributes in the range of 2 to 2.4% of their income to their church, while Catholic households contribute from 1 to 1.2%.

What does this mean in practical terms? It means that if Catholic households contributed at just the same rate as their Protestant friends, the same 2 to 2.4% of their income (we're not even talking about tithing here), the U.S. Catholic Church would receive something in the area of **$7 billion** a year more in annual revenues. This translates into about $400,000 per year for the average parish. What could a parish do with an additional $400,000 every year? Think of the deferred maintenance on the parish grounds that could be addressed. Think of the community outreach that the parish could perform. Think of improving on the scandalously low salaries that we currently pay our lay professional staffs. The list goes on.

But the news gets even worse. Not only are Catholics low financial givers, they also trail their Protestant friends in the amount of time they volunteer to their parishes. A study by Hoge et al. (1998) shows that the average Catholic household volunteered 1.6 hours per week to their church, while the average Protestant household in the study volunteered 3 hours per week — again, a two-to-one ratio.

What are the causes for the low giving, both in financial terms and as measured by volunteer time, that Catholic parishes receive from their parishioners? A number of studies are reviewed in Chapter Two that cite various reasons. But the fact of the matter is that introducing stewardship is probably the one best thing that a parish can do to increase members' contributions of their time, talent, and treasure.

The Meaning of Stewardship

The theology behind stewardship, as presented in the Bible, is straightforward. The master has departed on a trip and left the steward in charge. When he returns, the master asks for an accounting from the steward: "What have you done with what I entrusted to you?" The message is that all creation is a gift. Each of us has been entrusted with gifts, in the form of our time, talent, and treasure. Someday we will be called to give an accounting of how we used those gifts to advance the kingdom of God.

A number of thoughts come up frequently to describe stewardship:

- "All we have is really a gift from God, Who asks us to return a portion in the form of our time, talent, and treasure to support His work on earth."
- "Stewardship involves developing a need to give, rather than merely giving to a need."
- "Stewardship is an understanding of a total way of life; a conversion of mind and heart."
- "Stewardship is not about something we do, it is about who we are, and Whose we are."

Introduction

- "Stewardship is about asking ourselves, 'What do we own, and what owns us'?"
- "Stewardship is an act of worship, not an act of obligation."

In fact, stewardship is so much about what we as a Church should be preaching anyway that, even if the Church were flush with money and volunteer time, we should still emphasize the stewardship message.

In 1992, recognizing the emerging practice of stewardship at the time, the U.S. Catholic bishops thought it imperative to emphasize its theological foundations. They released a pastoral letter, *Stewardship: A Disciple's Response*. As the title indicates, stewardship is part of the Christian vocation of discipleship initiated at Baptism. As such, it is integral, not optional. Further, it calls on Catholics to be outward-focused, intent on serving all of humanity, but especially those with the greatest need. The bishops recognize that stewardship is costly and demanding to practice; in many ways, it is countercultural.

One reason why the bishops chose a theological, rather than prescriptive, approach to stewardship was to counter the notion that stewardship is only about money. This was partly in response to the common practice at the time (and still frequently employed today) of discussing stewardship once per year in the parish, in conjunction with a financial report and an appeal to parishioners to be generous so that the parish can meet its budget. The bishops hoped to make clear that stewardship is not a fundraising gimmick, but rather a spiritual conversion of mind and heart.

One of the primary supporters of stewardship in the United States has been the International Catholic Stewardship Council. Founded in 1962 as the National Catholic Stewardship Council (its subsequent name change reflected the reality of its membership), the primary goal of the ICSC has been to promote the concept of Christian stewardship. It does this through a number of venues, including the preparation and dissemination of stewardship materials, sponsorship of annual and regional conferences, and an Institute for Stewardship Development.

Through its programs, the ICSC offers both a vision of stewardship and practical aids to attain that vision. One such aid is its recently developed definition of stewardship, contained below in Table 1.1.

TABLE 1.1

International Catholic Stewardship Conference

Stewardship Definition

Stewardship is a way of living out our faith as individuals, as a faith community, indeed in the actions of our daily lives. Parish Stewardship refers specifically to those actions and attitudes that directly affect our parish community.

► First, as individuals, we strive to become Christian stewards as defined in the U.S. Bishops' Pastoral Letter, *Stewardship: A Disciple's Response*. The bishops state:

> A Christian steward is one who receives God's gifts gratefully, cherishes and tends them in a responsible and accountable manner, shares them in justice and love with others, and returns them with increase to the Lord.
>
> In other words, stewardship is making a choice to live a God-centered life. It means realizing that all we have and all that we are able to do are gifts from God, and that everything that we choose to do with those gifts is, in a sense, our gift back to God in gratitude. This is the way we fulfill our baptismal promise to love and serve the Lord. Stewardship is our way of responding to God's call with a life of gratitude.

► Second, the pastor, staff, parish leaders, and all parishioners seek to understand and embrace the three convictions which the U.S. Bishops say are foundational for stewardship:

- Mature disciples make a conscious, firm decision — carried out in action — to be followers of Jesus Christ, no matter the cost to themselves.
- Beginning in conversion, change of mind and heart, this commitment is expressed not in a single action, not even in a number of actions over a period of time, but in an entire way of life. It means committing one's very self to the Lord.
- Stewardship is an expression of discipleship, with the power to change how we understand and live out our lives. Disciples who practice stewardship recognize

> God as the origin of life, the giver of freedom, and the source of all they have and are and will be. They are deeply aware of the truth that "The Lord's are the earth and its fullness; the world and those who dwell in it." (Ps 24:1). They know themselves to be recipients and caretakers of God's many gifts. They are grateful for what they have received and eager to cultivate their gifts out of love for God and one another. (*Stewardship: A Disciple's Response*)
>
> ➤ Third, Christian stewards live out their discipleship through tangible practices of sharing their resources of time, talent, and treasure. This includes, but is not limited to, the following:
>
> - **Time.** All of our time should be God-centered, which means using our time to honor God. We should set aside a portion of our week to focus on strengthening our relationship with God through prayer, Mass, Scripture reading, and serving others.
> - **Talent.** We should assess our strengths and determine how they might be used to help build the kingdom of God. These strengths could be an overt talent like sewing or painting or an internal skill such as organizing or listening. Each of us is gifted and can perform some action to help others.
> - **Treasure.** Planning to return the first portion of our earnings to God is a way of showing our gratitude and commitment to stewardship. Tithing, giving the first 10% of what we receive, is the traditional (Biblical) guideline of how to give to God. Stewardship calls us to give in proportion to our blessings by sharing a percentage of our gifts. However, it also means being responsible stewards of the other 90%, or what is left, and using it in a way befitting a God-centered person if we are truly committed to embracing stewardship as a way of life.

As attractive as the concept of stewardship can be, it is often a tough sell in parishes when it is first introduced. Stewardship professionals caution that it takes at least five years for the concept of stewardship to take hold, and even then it must be regularly revisited as new parishioners move in and veteran parishioners need to be renewed.

One obstacle that must be overcome in introducing stewardship into a parish is the pride that parishioners typically take in their parish. Many parishioners are offended or insulted when told that, as good as their parish might be, transforming it into a stewardship parish can make it even better.

To help parishioners understand the difference between their parish — as wonderful as it might be — and a stewardship parish, I have developed a schematic (Table 1.2) to illustrate the difference between the two. While most would find a parish characterized by the left-hand column to be attractive, it could be argued that a parish demonstrating the characteristics in the right-hand column would be a far more effective parish at forming the discipleship of its parishioners.

The Plan of This Book

Stewardship can be a tough sell when first introduced into a parish, but a number of organizations stand ready to assist parishes wishing to begin or renew parish stewardship efforts. These include the International Catholic Stewardship Council, diocesan-level stewardship offices, and a large number of private consulting firms that will work with a parish one-on-one. In addition, there are scores of how-to books and handbooks on parish stewardship. Each of these provides a variety of practical activities (in most cases, breaking them out step-by-step) that a parish can employ to introduce or maintain stewardship. But which of these are effective and which not? Of those that are effective, which prove to have the greatest impact and be the place where a parish might place its priority? What are the best practices in parish stewardship activities?

The fact is that no one knows for sure. Anecdotal evidence — but no clear empirical support — exists. This book is intended to provide the first clear evidence to identify parish level stewardship activities that are effective, as opposed to those that intuitively sound like good ideas but in reality have no impact. In addition, it is the first book to empirically analyze all three elements of stewardship: time, talent, and treasure. Every other

TABLE 1.2

	A "Very Good" Parish	vs. A "Stewardship" Parish
Focus and Goals	To bring people into a relationship with our parish and with the work it does in a way that makes them want to support it.	To bring people into a closer relationship with God through the experiences of giving time, talent, and treasure that we help to create, by offering occasions where this giving is consciously evoked as a spiritual act and practice.
Ideal Outcomes	Parishioners make a contribution to the parish, in recognition that the parish needs resources if it is to continue its work — that is, parishioners "give to a need."	Parishioners are more generous in their gifts to the parish of their time, talent, and treasure because every gift becomes an occasion for, and a celebration of, growth in faith — that is, parishioners develop a "need to give."
Philosophical and Cultural Underpinnings	The philosophical and cultural root is philanthropy, "private action for public purposes." The intent is to encourage people to feel a commitment to the "common good of the parish," and voluntarily give of their resources — material goods that they feel they own — for the benefit of others.	The philosophical and cultural root of stewardship is a commitment to personal and collective behavior that recognizes and honors God's ultimate ownership of, and profound generosity in, all things. The intent is to encourage people to see all resources as gifts temporarily entrusted to us to be used and shared to promote the welfare of all of God's creation.
Ultimate Objective	To provide financial (and other) support for our parish, so that it may carry out the godly work to which we believe it has been called.	To "build the household of God" so there will be more human and spiritual, as well as material, resources to carry out the work of building the kingdom, in whatever form that work may take.

Adapted from Jeavons and Basinger, *Growing Givers' Hearts*

empirical study of stewardship has focused solely on treasure, or on time and talent, but not on all three.

The data that supports this study was collected under a grant from the Our Sunday Visitor Institute to the International Catholic Stewardship Conference. The ICSC, in turn, contracted with Villanova University's Center for the Study of Church

BEST PRACTICES IN PARISH STEWARDSHIP

Management to conduct the study. Survey items were suggested by the ICSC Stewardship Education and Services Committee — Scott Bader, Jim Kelley, Ed Loughlin, Lois Locey, and Julie Kenny.

A total of 1,459 parishes were surveyed: 474 were ICSC members, 985 were chosen randomly from the National Parish Inventory maintained by the Center for Applied Research in the Apostolate (CARA). (Of this latter group, 16 parishes were no longer in existence.) After two mailings, questionnaires were returned from 227 ICSC member parishes (48%) and 208 non-ICSC parishes (21%).

The ICSC member parishes were included to ensure a sizable sample of parishes that are actively pursuing stewardship. Thus, the sample of parishes that comprise this survey is not truly random, but weighted, and all results should be evaluated with that caveat in mind.

In addition to the survey, a series of focus groups of representatives of parishes were conducted nationwide. These focus groups were led by some of the aforementioned ICSC Committee members who advised the study.

Finally, it is important to emphasize what this book *is* and what it is *not*. It is not a how-to manual (e.g., how to set up a ministry fair, how to train a lay witness). As mentioned previously, there are plenty of organizational and print resources that do an excellent job of advising parishes on the specifics of each stewardship activity. Rather, the role this book plays is to cut through the anecdotal confusion and identify those stewardship activities that are likely to be most successful.

Following this chapter is a chapter that summarizes what researchers think they know about the effectiveness of various stewardship activities. That is followed by a discussion of parish demographic characteristics associated with contributions of time, talent, and treasure, regardless of the parish's stewardship efforts. The heart of the book is a series of chapters that analyze specific elements within broad categories of parish stewardship activities (the role of the stewardship committee, lay witness talks, parish communications, etc.). The book concludes with a chapter that identifies the eight most effective parish stewardship activities as they impact the **total** stewardship package: time, talent, and treasure.

REFERENCES

Greeley, Andrew M., and William McManus *Catholic Contributions: Sociology and Policy*. Chicago: The Thomas More Press, 1987.

Hoge, Dean R., Charles Zech, Patrick McNamara, and Michael J. Donahue. "The Value of Volunteers as Resources for Congregations." *Journal for the Scientific Study of Religion*, Vol. 37 (1998), pp. 470-80.

Jeavons, Thomas H., and Rebekah Burch Basinger. *Growing Givers' Hearts: Treating Fundraising as Ministry*. San Francisco: Jossey-Bass, 2000.

National Conference of Catholic Bishops/United States Catholic Conference. *Stewardship: A Disciple's Response*. Washington, DC: USCCB, 1992.

Chapter Two

PREVIOUS STUDIES

As mentioned in Chapter One, this book is unique in that it is an empirical study of all three dimensions of stewardship: time, talent, and treasure. Other empirical studies have analyzed one or the other of these (usually treasure), and it is instructive to learn what they have found. Other authors, using qualitative (non-empirical) approaches — usually firsthand observation — have identified the factors that they believe are important to a parish stewardship effort. The two research methods can be viewed as complementary to one another.

In this chapter, I look first at the qualitative study conclusions, followed by the quantitative study findings. These set the stage for the analysis that appears in the remaining chapters.

Qualitative Studies

Patrick McNamara

The preeminent stewardship researcher who employed qualitative techniques was the late Patrick McNamara. Patrick spent the latter part of the 1990s observing firsthand Catholic parishes and Protestant congregations with reputations for their stewardship, often visiting each more than once. He interviewed pastors, staff, stewardship committee leaders, and other parishioners. His work resulted in two books. *More Than Money: Portraits of Transformative Stewardship* described what he learned from the Protestant congregations. *Called to Be Stewards: Bringing New Life to Catholic Parishes* portrayed successful stewardship in Catholic parishes.

BEST PRACTICES IN PARISH STEWARDSHIP

From his visits, Patrick discovered that there are no shortcuts to becoming a stewardship parish. At a minimum it takes three to five years. Based on his experience, he was able to identify three distinct phases in a parish's stewardship journey (*Called to Be Stewards*, p. 110):

- Phase One: parishioners encounter the notion of stewardship.
- Phase Two: parishioners make stewardship choices, and based on those experiences, they seek to grow and develop a stewardship response.
- Phase Three: parishioners become fully engaged in discernment and stewardship, growing into a stewardship-based lifestyle.

Phase Three is not the end, but the beginning of lifelong response to be in a relationship with God.

Not surprising, Patrick found many similarities between successful stewardship Protestant congregations and successful Catholic parishes. One difference that he noted was that, because most Catholic parishes were relatively new to stewardship, they had the opportunity to learn from their Protestant neighbors.

Patrick's major findings, which he describes in detail on pages 162 to 166 of *Called to Be Stewards*, were the following:

- **The pastor's genuine, personal conversion to stewardship is key.** The pastor's commitment to stewardship, extending to his own pledging, enables him to overcome the natural reluctance and speak "frankly and fearlessly" about money. Stewardship cannot be delegated to the parish staff.
- **There is no such thing as a stewardship "cookie-cutter recipe" that fits all churches.** Parishes are distinctive from one another in history, demographics, personnel, and

membership. They need to tailor stewardship programs to their own situation.
- **Creation of a stewardship committee is vital to program success.** Stewardship will not work as an add-on to the parish pastoral council or finance council. A liaison with these committees needs to be maintained, but the stewardship committee needs to focus its full attention on setting and maintaining a stewardship vision for the parish. They are responsible for keeping stewardship out-front in the parish by incorporating it into every aspect of parish life.
- **Integrating stewardship themes into parish liturgies is vital.** This goes beyond ensuring that homilies periodically have a stewardship theme. Other elements of the liturgy, such as the hymns and the Prayers of the Faithful, also help to reinforce the awareness that stewardship is ultimately a spiritual journey.
- **Stewardship should be included in classes of the RCIA (Rite of Christian Initiation of Adults).** It is essential to impress upon all new members, both converts and newly arrived parishioners, the importance that the parish places on stewardship.
- **Stewardship is best envisioned as an invitation to be "prophetic."** Extending stewardship beyond the parish into the community helps to transform the parish.
- **Stewardship extends to parishioners' inner lives.** Stewardship is transformative. Through prayerful consideration of one's gifts, stewardship results not only in external activity but also in inner reflection.

Paul Wilkes

Another author who employed the qualitative approach was Paul Wilkes. Like Patrick McNamara, he visited Protestant congregations and Catholic parishes, observing them and interviewing key people in them. Unlike McNamara, however, Wilkes' interest was in identifying overall excellence, not just outstanding stewardship. But one parish that he studied — and which was profiled in his book *Excellent Catholic Parishes: The Guide to Best Places and Practices* — was St. Francis of Assisi in Wichita, KS. St. Francis of Assisi, of course, is nationally renowned for its stewardship emphasis, primarily due to the efforts of its former pastor, Msgr. Thomas McGread.

Msgr. McGread is internationally known for his work in transforming St. Francis of Assisi parish into the quintessential stewardship parish. Among its hallmarks are a tuition-free parochial school, perpetual adoration of the Blessed Sacrament, and a variety of social outreach programs. The success of St. Francis of Assisi has since spread throughout the diocese of Wichita — where all parishes practice stewardship — and to parishes across the country that have adopted the St. Francis of Assisi model.

Among the items of wisdom that Msgr. McGread shared with Wilkes were that he invites — never demands or requests — parishioners to enter into a stewardship way of life; also, that stewardship should be built upon "the three legs of any good parish":

- Prayer, including both liturgies and personal prayer
- Service, both to parishioners and to the community
- Hospitality to all

It is also important to avoid the temptation to go right to the treasure component of stewardship. Parishioners need to experience a conversion to the stewardship way of life. This is a gradual process, and they need to feel that this is their decision to make.

Wilkes concludes with a list of "18 Common Traits of Excellent Parishes" (pp. 157-67). All can be applied to stewardship parishes, but the traits especially relevant to stewardship that excellent parishes manifest are:

- The "habit of being." They are warm, welcoming places where parish life is spiritually rich and God-centered. Parishioners give of themselves willingly, not out of obligation or guilt.
- Innovative and entrepreneurial spirit. They see new and current needs and seek to meet those needs.
- A different kind of authority. The authority of both the pastor and the staff derives from reflective, sensible practice. Their leadership is anchored in both religious idealism and common sense.
- Being the center of parishioners' lives. The parish becomes the parishioners' base of operations, where they find strength and are reinforced by the actions of others.

Further, these parishes do not merely *allow* the laity to perform tasks that once were handled exclusively by clergy; they *encourage* (and expect) parishioners to go beyond usual assigned tasks and take on activities that might never have been done before.

These parishes also have spirituality at their core. Prayer is the core of not just their liturgies but also of all other parish activities. They realize that without a deep spirituality, even the best programs lack a crucial component.

Justin Clements

Although he is technically not a researcher, Justin Clements has written extensively on stewardship. His expertise comes from his experience as the Director of the Office of Stewardship and Development for the Diocese of Evansville, IN, and from the insights he has gathered as one of the more popular presenters at stewardship functions across the country. His "where-the-rubber-meets-the-road" analysis is especially helpful.

Among the books he has written is *Stewardship: A Parish Handbook*, which lays out from A to Z how a parish should go about introducing, and then renewing, stewardship. Although primarily a how-to book, Clements' parish handbook concludes with "Ten Characteristics of a Total Stewardship Parish" (pp. 199-200). Many of these are consistent with the items identified by Patrick McNamara and Paul Wilkes. They include:

- **Public Commitment by Parish Leaders.** This needs to be reflected in the parish mission statement and long-range plan.
- **Active, Dynamic Stewardship Conversion Committee.**
- **Year-Round Spiritual Formation and Educational Activities.** Parish education and formation activities remind all parishioners of their discipleship responsibilities at home, in the workplace, and in the community.
- **Annual Time, Talent, and Treasure Renewals.** Parishioners are compelled to share their gifts as a faith response.
- **Total Stewardship Financial Plan.** Elements include:
    - Envelopes used by all parishioners, including children
    - The promotion of tithing or proportional giving as the norm
    - Movement toward eliminating all second and special collections
    - All capital campaigns conducted according to teachings on stewardship
    - Planned gifts and endowments placed with the diocesan foundation
    - No school tuition
    - Parish publishes monthly budget updates and an annual accountability report
- **Contribution to Other Parishes.** The parish not only supports external causes financially, but encourages parishioners' time and talent contributions outside the parish.
- **Comprehensive Communication System.** All parishioners are kept up to date regarding every aspect of parish

life. An important tool is a monthly newsletter sent to every parish household.
- **Aggressive Hospitality Programs.** Newcomers and visitors are welcomed, and parishioners are regularly acknowledged and thanked for their stewardship.
- **Total Prayer Life.** All liturgical celebrations are planned for and evaluated. Time is set aside for prayer at all parish events. Prayer and spiritual growth opportunities (such as Scripture study groups, Perpetual Adoration of the Blessed Sacrament, public recitations of the Rosary) are available throughout the week.
- **Value-Added Service Philosophy.** Opportunities are provided for structured feedback regarding needs that are, or are not, being met along with evaluation of liturgies and parish programs.

Quantitative Studies

Over the years, a number of researchers have collected data and analyzed the determinants of parish-level contributions of money and volunteer time. Though most of these studies have not been performed with the intention of studying stewardship, per se, in many cases, their findings can be instructive. As indicated previously, one limitation that all of these studies share is that their focus on only one component of stewardship — typically, treasure.

In my book *Why Catholics Don't Give . . . And What Can Be Done About It,* I looked at the "treasure" component. The findings were based on an analysis of nearly 2,200 Catholic parishioners who responded to a national survey, along with insights gathered from a series of focus groups. Among the findings consistent with every other study of religious giving was that dollar contributions were greater among wealthier and more educated Catholics (although not on a percentage of income basis) and when parishioners had a positive opinion of their pastor.

BEST PRACTICES IN PARISH STEWARDSHIP

In contrast, I concluded that low Catholic financial contributions could be explained by:

- **The lack of financial accountability and transparency in Catholic parishes,** which leaves many Catholics in the dark as to how their contributions are used.
- **The absence of consultative processes in Catholic parishes** that would provide parishioners with an input into parish decision-making and a sense of ownership in parish activities.
- **The large size of Catholic parishes,** which leads many Catholics to behave as "free-riders," assuming that other members of the parish will pick up the slack if they underperform in their giving. Their large size also makes it difficult for parishes to develop a sense of community.
- **Parish teachings on giving,** which typically focus on contributing to meet the financial need of the parish (a consumerist perspective) rather than on the theologically grounded teaching of stewardship.
- **The reluctance on the part of parishes to require a commitment on the part of parishioners through an annual pledge.** My data showed that 37% of Catholics who attend Mass regularly base their financial contributions decision on what is in their checkbook — that is, how much they can afford that week.
- **The inability to connect with high-income Catholics** (low givers, compared to their Protestant counterparts) and younger Catholics.

I found that parishes that preach a year-round, rather than occasional, stewardship message received larger financial contributions. Part of this process entails convincing involved parishioners that their activity is a ministry, not a mere volunteer activity. Evidence shows that parishioners who view their parish activities as ministries contribute more time to those ministries and are more dedicated to them. As a happy by-product, Fr. Thomas Sweetser, S.J., the noted parish consultant, has observed that every time parishioners view their activity as ministry, rather than volunteer activity, their financial contributions double.

In an earlier study that I coauthored with my Villanova colleague Suzanne Clain (1999), financial and time contributions to both one's church and other nonprofit organizations were analyzed. Our findings rejected the conventional wisdom that these were all substitutes for one another (e.g., more in one area meant less in another). Rather, we found that parishioners who contribute more money to their church also tended to contribute more volunteer hours as well. Moreover, households that contributed more time and money to their church were also more generous in their contributions of both time and money to nonreligious charities.

Finally, a study that I coauthored with Robert Miller and Robert Parfet (2001) analyzed the responses to a survey of 27,000 Catholic parishioners in the Philadelphia archdiocese. In this study, we focused our attention on parish-level characteristics. One of our observations was that parishioners contribute more when they believe their parish places a priority on helping those in need. We also found that the extent to which parishioners use Sunday envelopes was unrelated to the level of financial contributions: simply using envelopes is not a substitute for a well-designed pledging program.

These empirical findings offer support for investigating some of the parish-level stewardship activities analyzed in this book. In later chapters, we consider parish characteristics such as the number of households and parishioner income. We also look at factors such as parish financial accountability and transparency, parish community-building activities, parish teachings on the importance of making a financial commitment, parish outreach programs, and parish support for encouraging parishioners to be engaged in ministry rather than volunteer activity.

Stewardship Measures

As has been mentioned previously, this study goes beyond the single-dimension measures of stewardship employed in the previously cited empirical studies. Rather than focus just on financial contributions, or just on volunteer hours, this study analyzes the impact of parish stewardship activities on all three components of stewardship: time, talent, and treasure.

This raises the question as to how to measure each of these components. Table 2.1 summarizes the way in which each stewardship component was measured for the purpose of this study.

Measuring treasure is relatively straightforward. As with most studies, I measure it as regular parish offertory collections (i.e., excluding second or special collections) divided by the number of parish households, or average contribution per household.

There are some problems with this measure, however. The denominator (number of households) can be unreliable, since it includes all registered households. Some parishes are better than others at keeping their registration rolls accurate. Also, it doesn't account for the portion of those households that are registered with the parish but are inactive or, for whatever reason, choose to attend Mass at (and financially support) a different parish. Nevertheless, it is the common measure used by most studies of this type, which allows for comparisons across studies.

Time and talent can be more challenging to measure accurately. The consultants on the project from the ICSC committee felt that merely measuring volunteer hours was too narrow and failed to fully capture the spirit of time and talent contributions that we find in a true stewardship parish. So the committee settled on a threefold measure of time and talent. Each of these relied on the perception of the person completing the survey, typically the pastor or parish life coordinator.

One measure was the percentage of parishioners who volunteer for parish ministries. A second measure attempted to

TABLE 2.1
Parish Stewardship Outcomes

Outcome	Mean Value
I. Treasure — Per Household Regular Contributions	$517
II. Percent of Parishioners Volunteering Time	27.4
III. Parish Spirituality Index — Sum of the Percent of Parishioners Engaged in the Following Activities:	46.3
Regularly attend weekday Mass	
Regularly attend other liturgical celebrations (e.g., adoration, rosary)	
Regularly attend bible study groups	
Regularly attend small group retreats	
Member of small faith group	
IV. Sum of Parish Outreach Activities	3.34
Soup Kitchen	
Food Pantry	
Tutoring/Literacy Program	
Hospital/Nursing Home Ministry	
Prison Ministry	
Habitat for Humanity House	
Sister Parish	
Sister Diocese	
Hospice Program	
Community Advocacy	
Other	

get at time devoted to spiritual activities. We asked about the percentage of parishioners who regularly participate in five spiritual activities, including attending daily Mass; attending other liturgical celebrations (adoration, rosary, etc.); attending retreats; belonging to Bible study groups; and belonging to small faith-sharing groups. We constructed a "Spirituality Index" by merely adding these percentages together. This, of course, can be a crude mea-sure. For example, one could imagine a devout parishioner who participates in all five activities. This person would count the same as five parishioners, each of whom participates in only one activity. But it captures the spiritual time element that the committee thought was critical.

Another time/talent measure that they thought was critical was time and talent spent in parish-sponsored outreach programs. Both Patrick McNamara and Justin Clements explicitly, and Paul Wilkes implicitly, recognize the importance of social outreach as part of the fabric of a stewardship parish. Our survey asked about ten social outreach ministries that the parish might be involved with. Some of these, such as sponsoring a sister parish or a sister diocese, might involve nothing more than writing a check. But the committee felt that all of them, when taken together, serve as good proxies for a measure of a parish's time and talent commitment to the community. The other activities included sponsoring: a soup kitchen; a food pantry; a tutoring/literacy program; a hospital/nursing home ministry; a prison ministry; a Habitat for Humanity house; a hospice program; and community advocacy. An "Outreach Index" was created by calculating the number of these activities in which the parish was engaged.

It should be observed that in many ways, these measures understate the case. For example, the Spirituality Index fails to adequately account for time spent in private prayer. Likewise, the measure of parish outreach understates the case by including only outreach specifically sponsored by the parish. Many parishioners, motivated by a sense of stewardship, perform outreach activities — including some of those mentioned here — on their own, outside of parish-sponsored programs. The individuals completing the survey would most likely not be familiar with all of the outreach activities undertaken by individual parishioners.

One particularly tough problem with these outcomes is that they are all measured in different units: dollars, percentages, and averages. This makes it very difficult to make comparisons across stewardship outcomes. To mitigate that problem, I developed a standard unit of measure by dividing each parish's outcome in each category by the average for that category. That is, I divided each parish's contributions per household by the average contributions per household for the entire sample of parishes ($517). Likewise, I divided each parish's percentage of volunteers by the average for the entire sample (27.4%); its Spirituality Index by the average (46.3); and its Outreach Index by the average for all the parishes in the sample (3.34).

By doing this, I've converted each parish's outcome into a comparison between it and the average value for all the parishes in the sample. An index value of 1 (one) for any outcome indicates that parish was right at the average of all of the parishes in the sample for their performance in that outcome. An index value greater than 1 demonstrates that they were above average; an index value less than 1 indicates that they were below average. For example, let's say that Parish A's Treasure Index is greater than 1.00 — for example, 1.20. That tells us that its treasure (contributions per household) is 20% greater than the average (that is, $620). An Outreach Index less than 1.00 — say, .95 — would indicate that parish's outreach is 5% less than the average (that is, 3.17). This allows us to compare stewardship outcomes across the various categories.

In the analysis that follows, each parish stewardship activity is evaluated for its impact on each of four measures of parish stewardship outcomes.

A Word about Statistics

The findings in this book are based on conventional social-scientific research. The key issue is that of "statistical significance." This refers to the fact that some observed relationships that apparently represent a pattern might in fact just be the result of chance occurrences. We want to be as certain as possible that our results represent fact, not accidental occurrences. In other words, we want them to be statistically significant.

The standard that most social scientists use to establish statistical significance is that they want to be at least 95% certain that their findings are accurate (one can never be 100% certain) and would likely occur again in the future. That is, their goal is that there is a 5% or less chance that their results are due to some random factors. Complex mathematical formulas are used to determine the level of significance of a particular relationship.

All of the findings described in this book have met the standard of statistical significance. That is, we can be at least 95% certain that the relationships reported are real and stable, and not a matter of chance occurrences.

A related issue is concerned with the direction of causality implied in a given relationship. It is a bit of a chicken-or-egg problem: does a particular activity lead to more stewardship in a parish? Or do parishes already ablaze with the spirit of stewardship reveal their zeal by undertaking a particular activity more frequently? For example, later in this book we will discuss the issue of incorporating stewardship into a parish's adult education programs. If this is found to be related to greater stewardship outcomes in a parish, is it because parish adult education programs that focus on stewardship lead to more stewardship? Or is it because parishes already heavily committed to stewardship ensure that their adult education programs contain that emphasis? The answer is probably a bit of both, that there is a "feedback" effect at work.

Furthermore, we can imagine a parish reaching a "tipping point" where an activity — like adult education emphasizing stewardship — then inspires parishioners to pursue a stewardship way of life. At some point (the tipping point), so many parishioners have been drawn to stewardship that the parish *becomes* a stewardship parish, and every activity (including adult education) reflects the parishioners' stewardship motivation. This is the ultimate goal.

Previous Studies

Although we might hypothesize some causality between particular parish stewardship activities and our measures of stewardship outcomes, the fact is that the best we can say is there is an "association," e.g., emphasizing stewardship in the parish's adult education offerings is **associated with** significantly greater levels of our stewardship outcomes. We can conclude, at a minimum, that these are the types of activities that successful stewardship parishes do — whether those activities caused the successful outcome, were a by-product of it, or some of both. That is worth knowing in and of itself.

Finally, I can't emphasize enough that the findings reported in this book are **averages**. Every parish is different. What works in one parish might not work in another. This book identifies stewardship tactics that were found to be, on average, successful in stimulating the desired stewardship outcomes. Readers need to filter these findings and decide how applicable they are to their particular parish situation.

REFERENCES

Clain, Suzanne Heller, and Charles E. Zech. "A Household Production Analysis of Religious and Charitable Giving." *The American Journal of Economics and Sociology*, Vol. 58 (1999), pp. 923-46.

Clements, C. Justin. *Stewardship: A Parish Handbook*. Ligouri, MO: Ligouri Press, 2000.

McNamara, Patrick H. *More Than Money: Portraits of Transformative Stewardship*. Washington, DC: Alban Institute, 1999.

———. *Called to Be Stewards: Bringing New Life to Catholic Parishes*. Collegeville, MN: The Liturgical Press, 2003.

Miller, Robert J., Robert A. Parfet, and Charles Zech. "The Effect of Life Cycle and Parishioner Perceptions on Average Household Giving in Catholic Parishes." *Review of Religious*

Research, Vol. 42, pp. 313-31. Hartford, CT: Religious Research Association, 2001.

Wilkes, Paul. *Excellent Catholic Parishes: The Guide to Best Places and Practices*. New York: Paulist Press, 2001.

Zech, Charles E. *Why Catholics Don't Give . . . And What Can Be Done About It* (Updated). Huntington, IN: Our Sunday Visitor, 2006.

Chapter Three

PARISH DEMOGRAPHIC AND SOCIOECONOMIC CHARACTERISTICS

Before we analyze the effectiveness of various parish stewardship activities, it is important to consider the impact of parish demographic characteristics. Due to the composition of their membership, some parishes might be predisposed toward higher or lower levels of time, treasure, and talent contributions, regardless of their stewardship efforts. Table 3.1 shows the relationship between parish demographic characteristics of the parishes in our sample and measures of each of the stewardship outcomes used in this study.

Recall that a number greater than 1.00 indicates an outcome in that stewardship component that significantly exceeds the average for the parishes in our sample. A number less than 1.00 reveals an outcome significantly less than the average in our sample. For example, a treasure coefficient of 1.10 tells us that parishes in our sample with that particular characteristic received 10% more financial contributions than the average parish in our sample. Meanwhile, a treasure coefficient of .95 would identify a characteristic that resulted in financial contributions that were 5% lower than the average in our sample. An asterisk indicates there was no significant difference between parishes with a particular demographic characteristic and those parishes without that characteristic.

TABLE 3.1
Impact of Parish Demographics

Parish Characteristic	Treasure	Volunteer Time	Spiritual Time	Outreach Time
GENERAL				
More than 1,750 households	.89	*	*	1.21
More than 40% college grads	1.15	1.09	*	1.16
More than 60% female	.73	*	*	.68
More than 20% of parishioners in parish for more than 5 years	*	1.11	1.16	1.13
AGE PROFILE				
More than 40% of adult parishioners age 35 or younger	1.11	*	*	*
More than 40% of adult parishioners age 60 or older	*	*	*	.93
More than 40% of households with children under age 18	*	1.15	1.11	*
SOCIOECONOMIC STATUS				
More than 20% of households income less than $25,000	.85	*	*	.84
More than 20% of households income greater than $100,000	1.14	*	*	1.18
RACIAL COMPOSITION				
More than 60% White	*	*	.89	*
More than 10% African-American	*	*	*	1.08
More than 20% Hispanic	.70	.85	*	*
More than 10% Asian	*	*	*	1.07

Parish Demographic and Socioeconomic Characteristics

General Characteristics

Based on the research presented in Chapter Two, some of the relationships shown in Table 3.1 are predictable. Larger than average parishes receive significantly lower financial contributions. There is a good reason for this shortfall: the "free-rider" effect. Individuals who belong to smaller parishes — say, 200 households — **know** that their contributions of time, talent, and trea-sure are critical to the parish's survival. Without everyone pitching in, the parish has no chance of succeeding. But parishioners belonging to a larger parish — say, 2,000 households — might be tempted to think to themselves that, with all these other parishioners contributing their time, talent, and treasure, the parish won't notice if they give less than they are capable of, or even nothing at all. The parish probably won't be affected when a few parishioners feel that way. But when many do (and there is a natural tendency in all of us to "free-ride"), the entire parish suffers.

Parishes with more highly educated parishioners receive significantly greater contributions, although that might be tied to the fact that more educated people tend to receive higher incomes. By the same reasoning, the lower than average treasure received by parishes with a large majority of adult females might reflect the lower income received by women in this country, especially women who are heads of households. Surprisingly, parishes with more long-term parishioners (members for more than five years) did not receive significantly larger financial contributions.

Moving away from treasure, parishes containing more highly educated adults were the beneficiaries of significantly more volunteer time, as were parishes with more long-term parishioners. Larger parishes, more highly educated parishes, and parishes with more long-term parishioners provided more outreach time, but parishes with a large majority of women contributed less outreach time. The only parishes associated with above-average time spent in spiritual practices were those with more long-term parishioners.

The fact that parishes with more long-term parishioners received greater than average contributions of volunteer time, spiritual time, and time spent in outreach is consistent with the findings of Patrick McNamara and others — that stewardship needs some time to take hold in a parish.

Age Profile

There are two separate theories on the impact that age would have on a parishioner's contributions of time, talent, and treasure: the life-cycle theory and the generational-cohort theory.

Life-Cycle Theory

The life-cycle theory is based on the presumption that societies change slowly, if at all. As people pass through different stages of their lives, they behave much like previous generations did at that same stage. In the context of their stewardship, younger households might be expected to contribute less. They have less discretionary income to contribute to their church; many of them are saving for a home (or paying on a mortgage) while at the same time, they're saving for their children's education and encountering child-rearing expenses and other costs faced by families just starting out. Their ability to contribute time and talent is also constrained by their child-rearing responsibilities. The exception would be in activities consistent with their child-rearing responsibilities — for example, teaching religious education, or being involved with parish-sponsored youth activities, such as scouts or youth athletic programs.

As they continue through their life cycle, middle-aged families are in a position to increase their stewardship. In many cases, they have their finances under control, and their child-rearing responsibilities have abated somewhat, freeing time to participate in parish ministries.

Senior citizens, many of whom are on a fixed income, might find it necessary to level off or even reduce their financial contributions. At the same time, they have more discretionary time, which allows them (health permitting) to contribute more time and talent to their parish.

Generational-Cohort Theory

The generational-cohort theory has been popularized by James Davidson and his colleagues (1997). It assumes that societies change rapidly, so that generations today might be totally different than earlier generations at the same stage. Davidson et al. have identified three (today, possibly four) generational cohorts in the U.S. Catholic Church: the pre-Vatican II generation, the Vatican II generation, and the post-Vatican II generation (which today might be divided into Generation X and the New Millennials).

The primary factor distinguishing generations is the historical circumstances during their formative years, generally ages 13 to 22. Different generations experience different historical circumstances and can be expected, therefore, to have different values.

For example the pre-Vatican II generation experienced their formative years during the Great Depression, World War II, and the Eisenhower Administration. This was a time when institutions (including the government and the Catholic Church) were generally well respected; this shapes their decision to support those institutions. For Catholics of this time period, the Church was present (in many cases central) in every aspect of their lives, including prayer in school. We would expect this generation to be relatively generous in its contributions of time, talent, and trea-sure to their church.

The Vatican II generation's formative years occurred during the 1960s and early 1970s. They were influenced by government activities such as the Vietnam War and Watergate, and by the dramatic changes experienced by the Catholic Church as a result of Vatican II and the reaction to *Humanae Vitae*. They take a more activist role in society, especially with regard to fighting injustice. They are more demanding of their Church, expecting both support for their activities and a larger role in Church decision-making processes.

Generation X and the New Millennials are similar to each other in that they were raised with a consumer mentality. They are much more influenced by popular culture and more indifferent to the roles that institutions, like the Church, play in their lives.

However, the pattern we found with respect to the impact of the age profiles of parishes and their stewardship outcomes is in many ways at odds with what we might have hypothesized from the previous discussion. For example, based on both the life-cycle and generational-cohort hypotheses, we would have expected lower financial contributions in parishes with more young adults — but those parishes received significantly more treasure. The life-cycle hypothesis would have predicted lower treasure in parishes with a greater proportion of older parishioners; while under the generational-cohort theory, we might have expected larger treasure from parishes with an older (pre-Vatican II) population. The fact that the treasure contributions index for this group was insignificant may be evidence that both factors are at work, but they tend to cancel each other out.

Parishes with more young adults did not receive significantly larger contributions of any of our measures of time and talent. This is consistent with the predictions of both the life-cycle and generational-cohort hypotheses. Parishes with older parishioners contributed significantly less outreach. This latter finding is consistent with the life-cycle hypothesis.

An interesting finding is the one related to the proportion of parish households with children under age 18. These parishes did not receive significantly higher levels of treasure and outreach contributions, consistent with both the life-cycle and generational-cohort hypotheses. But they did receive significantly larger amounts of volunteer time and spiritual time. Presumably, much of this time is related to family-rearing responsibilities. For example, as noted above, the volunteer time could be the result of time spent as religious education teachers or involvement with parish-sponsored scouts or athletic teams. The spiritual involvement could be the result of parental involvement in sacramental preparation with their children, such as attending retreats or daily Mass. It is up to the parish (perhaps through its stewardship efforts) to ensure that these activities are nourished and continue, even after child-rearing has ended.

Socioeconomic Characteristics

Income and wealth are always important considerations when discussing stewardship. Those studies that have analyzed the treasure component of stewardship have uniformly found that households with greater levels of income contribute more to their church, regardless of religious affiliation. But those same studies have found that financial contributions do not increase proportionately with income. In other words, high-income households contribute more dollars, but a lower percentage of their income, than do low-income households.

The pattern is even more pronounced for Catholics. Earlier, I had mentioned that, on the average, Catholics give about half as much as their Protestant friends. But in *Why Catholics Don't Give*, I found that among those households earning $100,000 or more annually, Protestants contribute more than **three times** as much.

What can be done to motivate high-income Catholics to become better stewards? Why are Protestants more successful with these "high-capacity" givers? What can we learn from them?

In an article that appeared on the Web site of the Leadership Network, titled "Disciplining the High-Capacity Giver,"

BEST PRACTICES IN PARISH STEWARDSHIP

Alexis Wilson quotes Todd Harper, executive vice-president of Generous Giving:

> We have to emphasize what we want *for* people, not what we want *from* them, and we have to be patiently persistent with them and recognize they are on a journey. We all are.

Later in that same article, Harper advises tapping into the parishioners' passions: "In the beginning, try to discern where they are and what gets them excited, and try to get them connected to a peer with passions in the same area." He believes that peer influence can be a very powerful motivator.

Finally, Harper observes that high-capacity givers are more likely than others to be concerned about the "return on investment" of their contribution. He emphasizes the importance of the parish communicating a vision and demonstrating accountability in their use of the funds.

A role model for high-capacity givers, according to Wilson's article, is Joseph of Arimathea. Joseph, a man of influence, was the only person who could ask for Jesus' body. He was wealthy enough to arrange for a burial. He also owned the tomb. He played a critical role in the Resurrection narrative. Clearly, there was a divine reason as to why he was well off financially!

The analogy is that some in our parishes are "Josephs" or "Josephines." They are blessed so that they can be a blessing. The challenge we face is to recognize the Josephs and Josephines in our parishes — including helping them recognize themselves! — and assist them in their faith formation.

We don't have information on individual household income in the data that supports this study. All we have is an indication of how many households have high incomes versus low incomes. Predictably, parishes with many high-income families receive larger than average treasure contributions. Likewise, parishes with many low-income families receive lower than average financial contributions. A similar pattern emerges with respect to parish outreach activities.

Ethnicity

Relatively few patterns emerged from an analysis of the impact of ethnicity on stewardship.

One was the fact that parishes with a predominantly White population did not receive significantly more contributions of treasure, volunteer time, or outreach time. But parishes with a large majority of White parishioners were significantly **less** likely to generate time spent in spiritual practices.

Parishes that had more than 10% either African-American or Asian parishioners were significantly more likely to be engaged in outreach activities, although there were no significant differences in any of the other stewardship measures. This could be the result of a greater sense of the importance of community among these ethnic groups.

Parishes whose population was more than 20% Hispanic received significantly **lower** contributions of treasure and volunteer time. It has been hypothesized that this is a cultural phenomenon; many Hispanics are immigrants from countries where churches receive financial support from the state, so there is less emphasis on parishioners supporting their parish with their time and treasure. A parish with a high percentage of Hispanics might need to adjust its stewardship approach to account for this cultural factor.

Summary

Clearly, a parish's demographic and socioeconomic situation will play a role in determining the success of its stewardship activities. But within the limits set by these characteristics, there are a number of activities that parishes can use to form their parishioners as good stewards. The remainder of this book analyzes the effectiveness of those activities.

REFERENCES

Davidson, James D., Andrea S. Williams, Richard A. Lamanna, Jan Stenftnagel, Kathleen Maas Weigert, William J. Whalen, and Patricia Wittberg. *The Search for Common Ground: What Unites and Divides Catholic Americans.* Huntington, IN: Our Sunday Visitor, 1997.

McNamara, Patrick H. *Called to Be Stewards: Bringing New Life to Catholic Parishes.* Collegeville, MN: The Liturgical Press, 2003.

Wilson, Alexis. "Disciplining the High-Capacity Giver." From the Web site of the Leadership Network; www.leadnet.org/downloads/High%20Capacity.pdf. Download date: November 15, 2007.

Zech, Charles E. "Generational Differences in the Determinants of Religious Giving," *Review of Religious Research*, Vol. 41, pp. 545-59. Hartford, CT: Religious Research Association, 2000.

———. *Why Catholics Don't Give . . . And What Can Be Done About It* (Updated). Huntington, IN: Our Sunday Visitor, 2006.

Chapter Four

THE ROLE OF THE STEWARDSHIP COUNCIL

The studies that we reviewed by Patrick McNamara, Paul Wilkes, and Justin Clement clearly established the importance of the pastor buying into stewardship and taking a leadership role in its implementation in the parish. Next to the pastor, it is generally believed that the most important actor in determining a successful stewardship effort in a parish is the parish stewardship council. Note the use of the term "council" rather than "committee." The group charged with creating and maintaining stewardship in a parish should be considered more than a committee. It should rightly be viewed as one of the pastor's key advisory councils, on a par with the parish pastoral and finance councils.

In their companion volume to the tenth anniversary of the pastoral letter *Stewardship: A Disciple's Response*, titled "Stewardship and Development in Catholic Dioceses and Parishes: A Resource Manual," the U.S. Catholic bishops address the issue of leadership:

> The personal commitment of the bishop or pastor is absolutely necessary for the success of diocesan and parish stewardship and development efforts. In addition, wherever possible, parishes and dioceses should have active stewardship committees whose members include a representative group of pastoral and lay leaders willing to pray, discuss, learn, and lead.

The stewardship council is the group charged with creating a stewardship vision for the parish, impacting the parish culture.

Their role is to bring the concept of stewardship to life in the parish.

Membership

In its manual *Stewardship: Disciples Respond — A Practical Guide for Pastoral Leaders*, the International Catholic Stewardship Council has identified the characteristics of those who are called to serve on the parish stewardship council (pp. 14-15). Ideally, they

- **Are spiritually motivated.** Their primary interest should be in forming parishioners' spiritual lives, not raising money for the parish.
- **Exemplify and live out stewardship.** Members should be recognized as individuals who live a stewardship way of life, even though they may not call it that. They are involved in the parish and are generous financial supporters.
- **Envision where stewardship can take the parish.** Members need to have a vision of what the parish could be and how stewardship could help get it there.
- **Are comfortable talking about money.** Eventually, the council is going to have to deal with the treasure component. The council's role will be even more critical in those parishes where the pastor is reluctant to address the topic of money.
- **Are willing to implement accountability in aspects of stewardship.**
- **Have personal qualities that contribute to success.** Council members should be organized, creative, and able to carry out their assignments.

The stewardship council is responsible for a variety of activities that help form a stewardship parish. Many of these activities are discussed in the succeeding chapters of this book: recruiting and training lay witnesses, organizing the parish ministry fair, ensuring that parish education programs at all levels contain a stewardship module, communicating about stewardship with parishioners, leading the pledge drive, and so on.

At times, the stewardship council might find itself in tension with the parish finance council. Members of the finance council, concerned with meeting the parish budget and convincing parishioners of the importance of "giving to a need," might not have patience with a program whose intent is to develop a long-term "need to give" among parishioners. Finance council members may be enamored of fundraising projects, which can run counter to the stewardship ideal and even confuse parishioners about the place of treasure in the parish.

For this and a variety of other reasons, most stewardship professionals strongly urge that the stewardship council stand as a separate body, not as a subcommittee of the parish pastoral council or the parish finance council. That being said, both our survey and our focus groups found a variety of organizational arrangements for parish stewardship councils. Here are some of the comments that emerged from our focus groups:

- "Stewardship in my parish is the job of our finance committee. It is somewhat one-dimensional as a result, dealing mainly with treasure."
- "Our stewardship committee is one of the important leadership groups in our parish, but they are not the only leadership group, and that sometimes makes stewardship more complicated and more difficult to achieve."
- "The committee consists of five couples, two of which are members of the parish council, and the stewardship committee is considered to be an extension of the parish council."
- "The stewardship council is the parish council."
- "The stewardship committee is responsible for the time and talent aspects of stewardship only."

- "It is one of six commissions reporting directly to the pastoral council."
- "Our new pastor has put the stewardship committee at the forefront. He views us as maybe even more important than the pastoral council and the finance committee. That has made all the difference."

Survey Findings

In our survey, 56% of the parishes indicated that they had a stewardship council or committee. Of these, 64% were stand-alone councils. Another 20% either overlapped with or were a subcommittee of the parish pastoral council, while 7% identified themselves as either the same as or a subcommittee of the parish finance council. There was a scattering of other organizational structures.

Does it make a difference what organizational form the stewardship council takes? Not really.

Table 4.1 shows the impact of a variety of factors associated with the parish stewardship council on the four measures of stewardship outcomes used in this study. Remember, the numbers report the impact relative to the average value of the measure in our sample. So, for example, a value of 1.20 for the treasure component would indicate an activity that resulted in parish treasure 20% greater than the average treasure in our sample ($517). An asterisk indicates an activity that had no significant impact on that stewardship measure.

We first asked if a parish had a stewardship committee or council. As Table 4.1 indicates, parishes with stewardship committees or councils in place (no matter what their organizational arrangement) generated significantly more treasure (12% more), volunteer time (7%), and outreach time (18%). Those that were organized as a separate council received more treasure (22%) and more outreach (20%). Those that were the same or a subcom-

TABLE 4.1
Impact of Stewardship Council

ACTIVITY	Treasure	Volunteer Time	Spiritual Time	Outreach Time
Parish has a Stewardship Council (56%)	1.12	1.07	*	1.18
Stewardship Council is a separate committee (64% of those with a Stewardship Council)	1.22	*	*	1.20
Stewardship Council is a subcommittee of the PPC (20% of those with a Stewardship Council)	*	*	*	*
Stewardship Council is a subcommittee of the PPC (7% of those with a Stewardship Council)	*	*	*	.95
Stewardship Council 7 years or more (36%)	1.27	*	*	*
Stewardship Council Meets Monthly (53%)	*	*	*	*
Pastor Frequently Attends Stewardship Council Meetings (79%)	*	*	*	*
Council has an annual plan (63%)	*	*	*	*
Council Education/Formation Activities				
Council has read Stewardship: A Disciple's Response (77%)	*	*	*	*
Council has studied other stewardship materials (80%)	*	*	1.20	*
Council has attended stewardship retreats (24%)	*	*	*	*
Council has attended diocesan or regional stewardship days (71%)	*	*	1.06	*
Council has attended ICSC Conference (52%)	*	1.15	1.11	1.31
Council has engaged in 3 or more Education/Formation Activities (Average 3.1)	*	*	*	1.24

mittee of the parish pastoral council had no impact on any of the stewardship outcomes. Those parishes that had somehow folded their stewardship committees into their parish finance council not only failed to experience a significant increase in any of the stewardship measures, they suffered a 5% **decrease** in outreach. But none of the organizational forms had a significant effect on volunteer time or spiritual activities.

It is important that all three groups — stewardship council, pastoral council, and finance council — work together. One solution is to have members from the various groups sit as liaisons and attend the other organizations' meetings to ensure adequate information. But in general, the exact organizational form that the stewardship council took was found to be of minor importance.

What about other characteristics on the stewardship council? Surprisingly, three factors were found to have no impact at all on any of our measures of parish stewardship outcomes. They were: the frequency of council meetings; the extent to which the pastor attends the meetings; and the issue of whether or not the council develops an annual plan (although 63% of the parishes in the sample indicated that their stewardship council did have an annual plan).

One characteristic of the council that played a relatively minor role was the length of time it had been in existence. Parishes in which the stewardship council had been in place for a longer period of time (seven years or more) generated significantly more treasure than the average parish in our sample. However, longer-serving stewardship councils had no impact on our other outcome measures.

It is important that stewardship councils, like all parish organizations, regularly participate in education and formation activities. In our survey we asked about five typical council developmental activities. Two, studying the Bishops' pastoral letter (77% of the committees had read it) and attending stewardship retreats (24% had attended at least one), had no impact on any of our stewardship outcome measures. The only education/formation activity that affected more than one outcome measure was attending the annual ICSC conference. This activity led to significantly higher outcomes in all stewardship measures except trea-sure. It might be noted that attending the ICSC conference, along with attending diocesan or regional stewardship conferences, were the only stewardship council activities that significantly impacted the parish's spiritual time. It might be that such conferences emphasize the spiritual dimensions more than any of the other activities listed.

Summary

Nearly every stewardship professional has emphasized the critical role that the stewardship council plays in creating and maintaining the vision of stewardship in a parish. Most of the key stewardship initiatives either come from, or are directly performed by, members of this council. For that reason, it is imperative that the right people, those who understand stewardship and live it in their daily lives, are selected to serve on this council.

Despite the importance placed on the characteristics of the stewardship council, our empirical testing found relatively few areas in which the council's characteristics had a significant impact on stewardship outcomes. The frequency of its meetings, the extent to which the pastor attends the meetings, and council formation activities like studying the Bishops' pastoral letter or attending retreats all failed to significantly affect even one stewardship outcome. Having a stewardship council is important, and there is some slight evidence that its organizational structure (i.e., best to serve as a stand-alone council) makes a difference, but otherwise the characteristics of the stewardship council itself were of only minor importance.

REFERENCES

Stewardship: Disciples Respond — A Practical Guide for Pastoral Leaders. Washington, DC: International Catholic Stewardship Council, 2004.

U.S. Conference of Catholic Bishops. "Stewardship and Development in Catholic Dioceses and Parishes: A Resource Manual," in *Stewardship: A Disciple's Response*, Tenth Anniversary Edition. Washington, DC: USCCB, 2002.

Chapter Five

LAY WITNESSES

One of the most important tasks of the parish stewardship council is to identify and train lay witnesses. Lay witnesses are individuals, couples, or — in some cases — entire families who are willing to stand before the parish community and testify to the impact that stewardship has had on their lives.

The U.S. Catholic bishops recognize the impact that a public witness to stewardship can make:

> Since stewardship is a way of life, and not simply a program of church support, the most important ingredient in any effort to encourage giving of time, talent, and treasure is the personal witness of individuals (clergy, religious, and lay) who have experienced a change of heart as a result of their commitment to stewardship. . . . To ensure that stewardship is seen as more than simply the parish's annual giving program, witness talks on stewardship themes should also be offered at various times throughout the year.

Witnessing the importance of stewardship in one's life is not an easy thing to do for most people. Care must be taken to select the right people, and then to train them.

Most lay witnesses are parishioners, although some parishes from time to time will bring in an outsider to serve as a lay witness. They motivate parishioners who can relate to the lay witnesses' stories and understand how stewardship can work for them. It's important to note that this presentation is not a plea for money or volunteers; it is about a real-life person's journey. It goes without saying, then, that it is essential for lay witnesses to have credibility with parishioners for the way they lead their lives. Their stewardship should be intentional and planned, so they can explain it to others, and should encompass all three components — time, talent, and treasure. Witnesses should be enthusiastic about their stewardship and comfortable in sharing that enthusiasm with others.

The ICSC publication contains many helpful tips on training lay witnesses. Among the "Dos" for lay witnesses, it mentions:

- Explain that stewardship means giving of the "first fruits," not what is left over.
- Stress the joy and fulfillment that comes to those who give God their first fruits.
- Talk about intentional, planned, and proportionate giving.
- Explain that it is important to give all three — time, talent, and treasure.

Among the "Don'ts," it stresses:

- (Not to) talk in bargaining terms.
- (Not to) discuss church needs or budgets.
- (Not to) suggest that parish stewardship is an obligation.

We asked our focus groups about their experiences in utilizing lay witnesses:

- "We use witness speakers around the Commitment Renewal. Different speakers at different Masses. It takes a long time to get these speakers. We need to look for them throughout the year. Speaker effectiveness varies, and we need to screen them more carefully."
- "Our parish has them during the yearly renewal and occasionally at other times during the year. We require that they turn in their talks in advance (written), and we also publish them in the bulletin in subsequent weeks so those who weren't at Mass can read them."

- "For the treasure commitment, we do a witness presentation. We also use witness speakers in other areas besides stewardship (e.g., examples of what a good marriage is about)."

Is the use of lay witnesses an effective stewardship strategy? Yes. As Table 5.1 indicates, 54% of the parishes in our sample utilized lay witnesses at least annually, and they received significantly larger than average contributions **in all four of our stewardship outcome measures.**

Who Should Serve as a Lay Witness?

Who should serve as a lay witness, beyond meeting the general standards described previously? Every parish is different. Every parish has its own personality. Every parish has its own culture. Every parish will look for different demographic characteristics in its lay witnesses. But we did find some patterns.

Table 5.1 shows the effect of four demographic types of lay witnesses. Three of them have a significant impact on three stewardship outcomes, while the other — the use of ethnic presenters — affected two. Young families and youth had the greatest impact on treasure, whereas old families and ethnic presenters significantly affected spiritual activities.

Perhaps the most interesting finding in Table 5.1 is that leveraging lay witness demographic characteristics by utilizing a variety of demographic types can be a very effective strategy. Using two or more demographic types significantly increased the outcome for treasure, volunteer time, and outreach time. Again, however, every parish is different. Each parish needs to invite lay witnesses from demographic groups that make the most sense for it.

Though most parishes use their own parishioners as lay witnesses, from time to time they might want to bring in someone from the outside to give a lay witness presentation. This is

TABLE 5.1
Impact of Lay Witnesses

Activity	Treasure	Volunteer Time	Spiritual Time	Outreach Time
Lay Witness Annually or More Often (54%)	1.11	1.09	1.11	1.17
WHO SHOULD SERVE AS LAY WITNESS				
Young Families (57% of those using lay witnesses)	1.16	1.15	*	1.25
Old Families (50% of those using lay witnesses)	*	1.18	1.09	1.28
Youth (30% of those using lay witnesses)	1.17	1.12	*	1.35
Ethnic (17% of those using lay witnesses)	*	*	1.28	1.35
Two or More Types of Lay Witnesses (Average 1.5)	1.15	1.18	*	1.27
Parishioners (100% of those using lay witnesses)	1.11	1.09	1.07	1.19
Guest Lay Witnesses (41% of those using lay witnesses)	*	1.18	1.29	1.20
MOST APPROPRIATE TIME				
Before Mass (9% of those using lay witnesses)	*	*	*	1.27
After Homily (67% of those using lay witnesses)	*	1.11	*	1.25
After Communion (48% of those using lay witnesses)	*	*	*	1.16
Not at Mass (17% of those using lay witnesses)	1.24	1.21	*	1.39
Use Lay Witness at More Than One Time Slot (Average 1.4)	*	1.15	*	**1.38**

Lay Witnesses

especially true for a parish that is just beginning its stewardship effort. Parishioners might not be familiar with the concept of serving as a lay witness and might be reluctant to step forward and volunteer for that role. Also, a guest lay witness might come with some built-in credibility.

In Table 5.1, we see that parishioners who serve as lay witnesses significantly increase contributions to all four of our stewardship outcomes. For the parishes in our sample, utilizing guest lay witnesses had a significant effect on three measures; it did not result in a significant increase in treasure. We can only speculate as to why this might be the case. Perhaps guest lay ministers, who are strangers to their audience, are reluctant to spend their limited speaking time talking about treasure. Or, they recognize the importance of establishing time and talent before treasure. Maybe, as outsiders, they lack credibility with parishioners who don't know them when they testify about stewardship and their own treasure contributions.

Whatever the reason, it is clear that using parishioners as lay ministers is a very effective tactic in developing stewardship across all four of our outcome measures.

When Should Lay Witness Talks Occur?

The question as to the timing of lay witness talks is a tricky one. Lay persons are not permitted to give the homily during Mass. Other times might be inconvenient. The options seem to be: before Mass; after the homily but before the Creed; after Communion; or at some time other than at Mass.

Our focus groups provided some insights on this issue:

- "Anything that seems to lengthen the Mass in any way is not very productive."
- "Special evening sessions about stewardship are poorly attended and do not seem to work."

The conclusions don't seem very promising!

According to our survey results, none of the three timing options connected to the Mass was significantly better or worse than any other point in the Mass. None of the three was associated with a significant increase in treasure or time spent in spiritual practices, although all four were associated with a significant increase in outreach efforts.

It's interesting to note that in spite of concerns about poor attendance at events held outside of Mass, in fact, that was the time that was most effective. Lay witness talks presented at parish functions other than Mass were associated with a significant increase in treasure, volunteer time, and outreach time.

Mixing and matching the time slots when lay witnesses are used had mixed results. According to Table 5.1, parishes that presented lay witness talks at more than one time slot received a significant increase in volunteer and outreach time. However, doing this had no effect on either treasure or spiritual time.

Summary

One of the best stewardship activities that a parish can offer is to present lay witness talks. While care must be taken in selecting the lay witnesses, and they must be properly trained, our results show that lay witness talks lead to significant increases in parishioner contributions to all four of our stewardship measures.

The question of which demographic is most appropriate led to mixed results, affirming the notion that all parishes are different and should select lay witnesses who best represent the parish's personality and style. There seems to be value in utilizing a variety of demographics to present lay witness talks.

Evidence also supports using parishioners to present lay witness talks, as opposed to using guests from outside the parish. Those parishes that used parishioners to give lay witness talks received significant increases in all four of our stewardship measures. Guest lay witnesses were effective in increasing three of our measures, but not treasure.

Finally, no particular part of the Mass was preferred to any other part in having a lay witness presentation. In fact, the most successful time was at an event other than Mass. Lay witness talks presented at these functions were associated with significant increases in three of the four stewardship outcome measures.

REFERENCES

Stewardship: *Disciples Respond — A Practical Guide for Pastoral Leaders.* Washington, DC: International Catholic Stewardship Council, 2004.

U.S. Conference of Catholic Bishops. "Stewardship and Development in Catholic Dioceses and Parishes: A Resource Manual," in *Stewardship*: *A Disciple's Response*, Tenth Anniversary Edition. Washington, DC: USCCB, 2002.

Chapter Six

OTHER PARISH STEWARDSHIP ACTIVITIES

This chapter considers the impact of a variety of other parish stewardship activities. The activities discussed in this chapter are intentionally directed at enhancing parish stewardship, unlike some activities discussed in subsequent chapters that might be present even in those parishes without a stewardship focus. Many of the activities described in this chapter would come under the purview of the parish stewardship council. Most involve a serious time commitment in planning the activity.

Homilies

Nearly every Sunday's Scripture readings present an opportunity for the homilist to preach on the topic of stewardship. After all, more than half of Jesus' parables were concerned with issues such as money or possessions — far more than the number of parables that focus on love. Apparently, Jesus thought that money or possessions are a greater threat to our salvation than a lack of love would be. Likewise, giving of time, talent, and treasure are frequent topics in St. Paul's letters and in the Acts of the Apostles.

No one would argue that stewardship should be the theme of the homily on *every* Sunday. But pastors and stewardship council members should know that a parish that is serious about stewardship will recognize that parishioners need reminders on a regular basis. Surely, stewardship needs to be preached on more frequently than once a year, in conjunction with the parish's annual Stewardship Sunday. In our survey, about 20% of the parishes indicated that stewardship was "seldom or never" the topic of the Sunday homily.

Are frequent homilies on stewardship effective? Yes. Table 6.1 indicates that those parishes in which stewardship is the topic of the homily six times a year or more (still a relatively low standard to meet) receive significantly greater contributions of time and talent in the form of volunteer hours, time spent in spiritual practices, and outreach activities.

The only stewardship measure unaffected by stewardship homilies was treasure. Perhaps this reflects the reluctance on the part of many homilists — in particular, priests — to preach on the subject of money and possessions. Dan Conway, in his two excellent studies (*The Reluctant Steward* and *The Reluctant Steward Revisited*), has pointed out that, for a variety of reasons, priests are hesitant to discuss money from the pulpit. John and Sylvia Ronsvale, in their book *Beyond the Stained Glass Windows*, found that only 6% of the pastors they surveyed agreed with the statement, "Most pastors enjoy preaching about money."

One of the primary reasons is the feeling on the part of many priests that seminary training has left them ill-prepared to speak authoritatively on the topic. Another is the concern that their celibate lifestyle causes them to lose credibility when they preach about money. Some might fear that talking about money will alienate their parishioners. As one focus group participant put it, "Having our priests preach about stewardship has not worked very well. They don't seem comfortable with it."

At the same time, communicating with parishioners on the role of money and possessions in their lives is an obligation of every priest. We wouldn't let a priest who was uncomfortable with making sick calls avoid that responsibility. So too, we need to impress upon our priests that preaching on the treasure component of stewardship is not an optional part of their priesthood.

TABLE 6.1
Other Parish Stewardship Activities

	Treasure	Volunteer Time	Spiritual Time	Outreach Time
PARISH STEWARDSHIP ACTIVITY				
Six or More Stewardship Homilies Annually (38%)	*	1.15	1.12	1.24
Ministry Fair (43%)	*	*	1.14	*
Commitment Sunday (62%)	*	*	1.07	*
SUPPORT OF TIME AND TALENT				
Gift Discernment (16%)	*	1.13	*	1.27
Ministry Commissioning (42%)	1.09	1.12	*	1.16
Ministry Appreciation Dinner (54%)	*	1.10	1.09	1.17
Two or More Support Activities (Average 1.2)	1.10	1.15	*	1.21
Stewardship a Part of Parish Plan (41%)	1.18	1.19	1.13	1.24

Ministry Fairs and Commitment Sunday

In many parishes, the highlight of the stewardship calendar is the annual parish ministry fair, often held in conjunction with a commitment Sunday. The intention of a ministry fair is to educate parishioners on the many opportunities to serve in a ministry in the parish. Typically, the parish stewardship council prepares a catalog, listing parish ministry opportunities and contact people, which is either mailed in advance or available at the fair. At the fair itself, ministries sponsor booths that describe their work and make ministry members available to answer questions. The ministry fair often coincides with the opportunity for parishioners to indicate their interest by making both a financial commitment and a commitment to join a particular ministry. Some parishes keep the two events separate, with the ministry fair held on one weekend and Commitment Sunday on a different weekend. In many of those parishes, Commitment Sunday involves the opportunity to commit to treasure contributions by completing a pledge card.

We asked our focus groups about ministry fairs and commitment Sundays. The reactions were mixed.

On Ministry Fairs:

- "We stopped conducting a ministry fair — the return did not seem to justify the effort."
- "We just did a ministry fair for the first time in two years. We'll keep doing it every year from now on, because we saw the drop-off when we didn't."
- "We have a problem with follow-up. There is no way of assuring that leaders are calling people after signup."
- "We started doing it in spring and fall, splitting the ministries between the two ministry fairs — those that need ministers ready before the fall (e.g., Religious Ed.) do it in the spring, and others do it in the fall."

Other Parish Stewardship Activities

On Commitment Sunday:
- "We did one Sunday for each in close succession. Time first, then talent, and finally treasure."
- "I think it's wrong to call it 'Commitment Sunday' because we never really ask for a commitment. We talk about stewardship and talk about commitment, but we never put the people in a position of having to commit. It is as if we are afraid we are going to offend someone. It is like we are embarrassed to challenge people too much."

As pointed out by one of the focus group comments, one of the most important components of a ministry fair or commitment Sunday is to ensure follow-up. One surefire way to dim the spirit of stewardship in a parishioner is to have that parishioner indicate an interest in a particular ministry, but then never to be contacted about it.

How effective are ministry fairs and commitment Sundays at forming parish stewardship? According to the data shown in Table 6.1, 43% of the parishes sponsor ministry fairs and 62% hold a commitment Sunday. Both ministry fairs and commitment Sundays are useful in generating more time spent in spirituality practices. They are ineffective, however, at promoting any of the other components of stewardship, including volunteer time and outreach activities. Perhaps this is not surprising. Nearly every scholar who has researched individuals' decisions to volunteer (to both religious and secular causes) has concluded that the most valuable tool is a personal invitation to volunteer (see Freeman 1997). In fact, the Independent Sector (2001) has estimated that 71% of all volunteers had been asked to do so.

This is not surprising to most parishioners. In some parishes, particular ministries are viewed as being controlled by a clique. An outsider in those parishes would be reluctant to volunteer without an invitation. At the same time, most parishioners would agree that it is difficult to turn down a personal request to join a particular ministry, especially if that request comes from the pastor.

While ministry fairs might be useful as education and communication tools to alert parishioners as to ministry opportunities in the parish, they are probably less successful in actually recruiting new members to join a particular ministry. They certainly are not nearly as effective as a personal invitation, especially if that invitation comes from the pastor. So, although ministry fairs have a role to play, any expectations about their value in promoting stewardship should be modest.

We have more to say about commitment Sundays in a future chapter, when we discuss the issue of pledging.

Support of Time and Talent

Another task typically entrusted to the parish stewardship council is to support those who are contributing their time and talent. The three most common types of support are assisting in gift discernment, holding a ministry commissioning ceremony, and sponsoring a ministry appreciation function. We asked about these three specifically in our survey and gave respondents the opportunity to indicate others if they desired.

Gift Discernment

As St. Paul has reminded us:

> Now, there are varieties of gifts, but the same Spirit; and there are varieties of service, but the same Lord; and there are varieties of working, but it is the same God who inspires them all in every one. To each is given the manifestation of the Spirit for the common good.
>
> — 1 Cor 12:4-7

Other Parish Stewardship Activities

Frequently, parishioners consider some ministries, such as those involved with the liturgy, to be more important than others, but the implication of St. Paul's letter is that all ministries are equally important. All of the gifts that parishioners possess are needed. What is needed is a discernment process to help parishioners identify their particular gifts and where these gifts can make the greatest contribution.

A critical aspect of a parish's stewardship effort is to assist each parishioner in discovering the ministry where their individual gifts are most suited. In many ways, allowing parishioners to serve in the wrong ministry is worse than if they hadn't served at all.

There are a variety of methods that parishes can use to support parishioners in their gift discernment process. One example is the TAP© method developed by Paul Wilkes for his three-part parish stewardship formation program, *New Beginnings*. The TAP© method helps parishioners determine the ministry for which their gifts are most suited by asking them to self-analyze their

- Talent — discover the natural and spiritual gifts that God has uniquely bestowed on them
- Aptitude — analyze their personal style of doing things
- Purpose — discern where God is pointing them to serve

The TAP© method includes a series of questions under each of these three categories that are meant to lead parishioners to discover the types of ministries for which they are best suited. Parishioners are asked to rate themselves for each question on a six-point scale ranging from "Never" to "Yes, very much so."

Table 6.1 shows that only about a sixth of the parishes in our sample assisted parishioners with gift discernment. As might be expected, based on the findings presented in Table 6.1, parishes that utilize some form of gift discernment experience significantly more volunteer time and outreach activities. Treasure and time spent in spiritual practices are not significantly affected.

Ministry Commissioning

A second activity that would be supportive of contributions of time and talent is a special ministry commissioning ceremony. Often held as part of the Sunday liturgy, a ministry commissioning ceremony provides public witness to the importance of stewardship of time and talent in the parish. This not only serves to recognize and encourage those engaged in ministry, it also provides an opportunity for other parishioners to reflect on their own contributions of time and talent.

Table 6.1 shows that 42% of the parishes in our sample employed some form of a ministry commissioning ceremony. From Table 6.1 we see that, like gift discernment, a ministry commissioning ceremony is associated with significantly greater levels of parish volunteer time and outreach activity. However, unlike gift discernment, it is also related to larger contributions of treasure. A ministry commissioning ceremony can also be an occasion for parishioners to reflect on other components of their stewardship.

Ministry Appreciation Dinner

Finally, a parish might choose to recognize all those parishioners who have served a ministry in any capacity by holding a general thank-you function such as an appreciation dinner. Although this seems consistent with a sense of Christian gratitude, the concept has some detractors. They point out that, through our Baptism, we have not only a right but also a responsibility to participate in a ministry; therefore, thanking someone for merely carrying out their responsibility strikes them as unnecessary and perhaps even counterproductive. Thanking those who engage in a ministry might lead them to think that their participation is a volunteer activity, not a ministry.

Perhaps a better way of viewing any ministry appreciation function is not as a thank-you, but as an act of affirmation. Inviting those engaged in a ministry to the function is not meant to convey the message, "Thank you for doing something that you did not have to do." Rather the message is one of affirmation, "What you do is very important to the life of this parish." It is important that the right message as to why the appreciation function is being held is properly conveyed.

Ministry appreciation dinners were the most popular method of supporting time and talent among parishes in our sample, with more than half holding them. Sponsoring a ministry appreciation dinner, as indicated in Table 6.1, has the anticipated result of leading to higher levels of parish volunteers and outreach activities. But it is also associated with greater participation in parish spiritual activities.

Unfortunately, 19% of the parishes in our sample indicated that they did nothing to support contributions of time and talent. Sponsoring each of these activities individually, as Table 6.1 reveals, can lead to significant increases in various measures of parish stewardship outcomes. However, as the table indicates, parishes that sponsor two or more activities meant to support contributions of time and talent receive greater contributions in three stewardship measures. And, based on the value of the coefficients, the increases in both treasure outcomes and volunteer time were greater than those received from the sponsorship of any one activity.

To sum up, supporting parish contributions of time and talent with such activities as gift discernment, ministry commissioning ceremonies, ministry appreciation dinners, and other similar activities can significantly influence stewardship contributions in areas other than just volunteer time and outreach activities.

Parish Planning

One of the themes of this book is that in order to be successful, stewardship must permeate the entire parish. This is most evident in the importance that stewardship plays in the parish planning process.

We asked our sample to indicate the extent that stewardship is incorporated into the parish's normal planning process. A minority, 41%, indicated that it was. Table 6.1 indicates that those parishes that specified that stewardship played a critical role in their parish planning received significantly larger contributions of all four of our stewardship outcomes.

The message is clear. Parishes that are serious about stewardship will ensure that their planning revolves around their identity as a stewardship parish.

Summary

This chapter has considered the effectiveness of a variety of common parish stewardship activities. In the process, some myths were exposed. Activities like ministry fairs and commitment Sundays in fact have no discernable impact on outcomes like the number of parish volunteers and outreach activities. While perhaps valuable in educating parishioners about the availability of ministry activities, they are not a replacement for a simple direct invitation to a parishioner to join a ministry.

Homilies on stewardship were found to be effective in stimulating all stewardship outcomes **except** treasure. This outcome is likely a result of priests' discomfort with preaching about money and possessions.

Supporting time and treasure with individual activities like gift discernment, a ministry commissioning ceremony, or a ministry appreciation dinner each were associated with greater stewardship outcomes. However, parishes that offered more than one type of time and talent support found that combining them was in some ways even more effective than the individual activities by themselves.

Finally, the finding that identifying stewardship as an important piece of the parish plan supports one of the themes of this book. In order to be successful, stewardship needs to permeate the entire parish life. Those parishes that demonstrate their commitment to stewardship by placing it at the heart of their parish plan receive significantly greater levels of all four of our stewardship measures.

REFERENCES

Conway, Daniel. *The Reluctant Steward Revisited: Preparing Pastors for Administrative and Financial Duties.* St. Meinrad, IN: St. Meinrad Seminary, 2002.

Conway, Daniel, Anita Rook, and Daniel A. Schipp. *The Reluctant Steward: A Report and Commentary on the Stewardship and Development Study.* Indianapolis, IN and St. Meinrad, IN: Christian Theological Seminary and St. Meinrad Seminary, 1992.

Freeman, Richard B. "Working for Nothing: The Supply of Volunteer Labor." *Journal of Labor Economics,* Vol. 15, pp. S140-S166. Chicago: University of Chicago Press, 1997.

Giving and Volunteering in the United States 2001. Washington, DC: Independent Sector, 2001.

Ronsvale, John L., and Sylvia Ronsvale. *Beyond the Stained Glass Windows: Money Dynamics in the Church.* Grand Rapids, MI: Baker Books, 1996.

Wilkes, Paul. *New Beginnings: A New Way of Living as a Catholic.* Distributed by St. Anthony Messenger Press, 2003.

Chapter Seven

PARISH FORMATION AND EDUCATION PROGRAMS

As has been repeated frequently, one of the themes of this book, supported by the findings of Patrick McNamara, Paul Wilkes, Justin Clements, and others, is that to be truly effective, stewardship must permeate the entire life of the parish. One opportunity for ensuring that stewardship inculcates the entire parish is through the parish's ongoing formation and education programs.

In their document "Stewardship and Development in Catholic Dioceses and Parishes: A Resource Manual," the U.S. Catholic bishops recognize the importance of ongoing stewardship education and formation.

> With the assistance of his stewardship committee, the bishop or pastor should establish a series of educational initiatives at the diocesan and parish levels that would encourage **all** members of the Catholic community . . . to meditate on stewardship themes and to pray for the grace to follow Jesus as mature Christian disciples, without counting the cost. . . . Dioceses and parishes serious about making stewardship a way of life for individuals, families, and communities of faith will include stewardship themes in all adult formation and education programs. . . . Opportunities for learning about (and sharing) their gifts of time, talent, and treasure should be integrated into all educational and formation activities sponsored by parishes, schools, and dioceses

for youth. . . . The lifelong process of stewardship education and formation begins at home in the domestic church and extends to parish and school religious education programs (emphasis on p. 73 added).

In our survey, we asked about the extent to which stewardship and the language of stewardship are included in a variety of formation and education programs offered by the parish. The results appear in Table 7.1.

Youth Programs

Most parishes offer an array of religious education programs for their children and teenagers. Many sponsor a parochial school, either on their own or in cooperation with neighboring parishes. Nearly all offer religious education for students who are not enrolled in a parochial or private school. A good number of parishes try (with varying degrees of success) to offer formation and education programs for their high school youth. And, of course, most parishes take sacramental preparation seriously.

These formation/education programs provide an excellent opportunity to develop stewardship in a parish. Not only do they reach the children and introduce them to the possibilities that good stewardship offers, but they also provide an entrée to the parents. Parents who experience their children learning — and asking them — about stewardship might be more inclined to investigate it themselves.

A number of age-appropriate stewardship activities can be introduced in these programs. Parish envelopes could be distributed to encourage children to tithe their allowance. Classes could take on service projects that call on the children's time and talent. These could then be highlighted in the parish bulletin or newsletter. We saw in Chapter Five that having youths serve as lay ministers is also a very effective stewardship activity.

TABLE 7.1
Parish Stewardship Formation and Educational Programs

Parish Stewardship Formation/Educational Program	Treasure	Volunteer Time	Spiritual Time	Outreach Time
YOUTH PROGRAMS				
Parochial School (35%)	1.15	*	*	1.19
Religious Education/CCD (57%)	1.08	1.09	1.06	1.13
Youth Group (36%)	1.15	1.16	1.12	1.24
Sacramental Preparation (36%)	*	1.10	1.11	1.09
ADULT PROGRAMS				
Adult Education (46%)	1.09	1.14	1.09	1.19
Senior Citizen Group (15%)	1.29	1.22	1.25	1.35
RCIA (55%)	1.12	1.08	*	1.12
Spiritual Renewal (31%)	1.17	1.15	1.21	1.26
Three or More Stewardship Formation/Educational Programs (Average 3.1)	1.12	1.12	1.08	1.16

BEST PRACTICES IN PARISH STEWARDSHIP

Sacramental preparation is an especially opportune time for stewardship to be introduced to both parents and children. For example, time, talent, and treasure discernment is a most appropriate facet of the preparation for Confirmation. But the benefits can reach beyond the confines of the individual family: in some places, the entire parish is invited to become involved in sacramental preparation. This serves as an occasion for stewardship renewal for all parishioners.

We've listed only a handful of ideas here. For a fuller treatment, the reader is urged to consult the ICSC publication *Children's Stewardship Manual*.

So, how productive is it to incorporate a discussion of stewardship into the curriculum of a parish children's and/or teenagers' religious formation/education programs? Unfortunately, except for religious education, only a minority of parishes in our sample had stewardship as an element of these programs Still, as Table 7.1 shows, although the results are mixed, they're generally positive.

Stewardship education in parochial schools elicits greater contributions of treasure and outreach activities, but does not have a significant impact on contributions of volunteer hours or spiritual time. Sacramental preparation that incorporates a segment on stewardship is associated with larger contributions of volunteer time, spiritual activities, and outreach efforts, but not treasure.

On the other hand, integrating stewardship into both religious education and (notably) youth groups significantly impacts all four of our stewardship measures.

These findings stand in contrast with the results shown in Table 3.1 (see p. 36). In our discussion in Chapter Three, we noted that those parishes with a large number of families with children under 18 (presumably those involved in child and youth formation and education programs) received larger contributions of volunteer time and were engaged in more spiritual activities. But they were no different from other parishes in their treasure contributions or outreach activities. The fact that incorporating stewardship into the curriculum of both religious education and youth groups — and to a lesser extent, in sacramental preparation — leads to increases in all of our stewardship outcome measures speaks to the effectiveness of including stewardship in the formation/education of a parish's young people.

One interpretation of these findings is that providing stewardship education to children and teenagers serves to promote stewardship across the parish — that is, stewardship education causes good parish stewardship. On the other hand, it is difficult to attribute a parish's success at stewardship to the fact that they have been able to form their youngsters as good stewards, since these cohorts are unlikely to be big contributors of time, talent, and treasure. An alternative interpretation is that parishes that are already absorbed in stewardship are more likely to ensure that stewardship is an integral part of the curriculum; in other words, good parish stewardship causes stewardship education.

But perhaps the best interpretation is a combination of these. Parishes that are already dominated by the spirit of stewardship ensure that stewardship is an essential part of the religious education and youth group curriculum. This, in turn, serves to promote stewardship in the parish by inspiring children and youths — and, ultimately, their parents — to join the stewardship movement.

Adult Programs

Because adults are the primary contributors of time, talent, and treasure, the impact of stewardship formation programs for adults on parish stewardship outcomes is more direct. At the same time, though, we should expect a feedback effect where parishioners who have adopted a stewardship way of life will press for more stewardship formation opportunities.

As with youth programs, Table 7.1 shows that stewardship appears in a minority of adult education/formation activities with the exception of RCIA. At the same time, the data shown in Table 7.1 reveals that stewardship education for adults is extremely successful at eliciting greater levels in each of our mea-sures of stewardship outcomes.

We asked our sample about four adult-oriented stewardship formation activities: adult education, senior-citizen groups, evangelization through the Rite of Christian Initiation for Adults, and spiritual renewal programs. With the exception of RCIA programs, integrating stewardship into each of these formation activities was associated with greater contributions of treasure and volunteer activity and more involvement in spiritual and outreach activities. Incorporating stewardship into RCIA increased all of our outcome measures except spiritual activities. As an aside, it should go without saying that a parish that is serious about stewardship would make every effort to introduce the concept to all of its new members, whether they are converts coming through the RCIA program or newly arrived parishioners.

Many parishes struggle with adult education. In this day of busy two-earner and single-parent households, it is difficult for parishes to entice members to attend their adult education offerings. But this is one activity where a stewardship emphasis can play a significant role in increasing all four measures of stewardship.

One successful strategy is emphasizing stewardship in parish-sponsored senior citizens' events. The results in Table 7.1 concerning the effectiveness of senior citizens' stewardship formation programs are a bit surprising on two accounts.

First, as described in Chapter Three, it is not surprising that including stewardship in programs intended for senior citizens results in more volunteer hours and more participation in spiritual and outreach activities, since many of them are retired and have a bit more discretionary time to contribute. What is surprising is that it also results in greater contributions of treasure. Ordinarily, we would not expect a group of parishioners, many of whom are living on a fixed income, to be such successful stewards of trea-sure.

Second, not only does incorporating stewardship into senior citizens' programs bring about larger amounts of each of our measures of stewardship outcomes; for each outcome, **the increase is greater than for any other formation/education activity**. The increases range from 22% (for volunteer time) to 35% (for outreach activities). Even treasure contributions are 29% greater than the average of all parishes in the sample.

These findings stand in spite of the fact that the results presented in Table 3.1 and described in Chapter Three showed that, in general, parishes with more senior citizens received similar levels of treasure, volunteer time, and spiritual activities — and significantly **less** involvement in outreach activities — than average parishes in our sample. Clearly, based on the results shown in Table 7.1, emphasizing stewardship to this group has a dramatic impact.

Finally, in keeping with our theme of stewardship permeating the entire parish, Table 7.1 demonstrates that those parishes that incorporate stewardship into a multitude (three or more) of their formation/education programs (no matter what they were, youth or adult) received significantly greater levels of each of our stewardship outcome measures.

Summary

It is difficult to think of a parish as a stewardship parish if it doesn't emphasize the concept of stewardship in all of its formation/education programs. As I've frequently emphasized, to be effective, stewardship should permeate the entire parish. Clearly, this should start with formation/education programs.

As it turns out, incorporating stewardship into parish formation/education programs is extremely successful at increasing levels of all four of our stewardship outcome measures. This is true for both children and youth programs and for adult programs. Comparing the findings in this chapter (and the results shown in Table 7.1) with the findings reported in Chapter Three (results in Table 3.1 on page 36) reveals just how effective a stewardship component in parish formation/education programs can be. This supports the notion that stewardship is most effective when it pervades the entire parish.

REFERENCES

International Catholic Stewardship Council. *Children's Stewardship Manual.* Huntington, IN: Our Sunday Visitor, 2000.

U.S. Conference of Catholic Bishops. "Stewardship and Development in Catholic Dioceses and Parishes: A Resource Manual," in *Stewardship: A Disciple's Response,* Tenth Anniversary Edition. Washington, DC: USCCB, 2002.

Chapter Eight

PARISH TEACHINGS ON PARISHIONERS' LEVEL OF SUPPORT DECISIONS

One of the key factors in assisting parishioners in their stewardship journey lies in the parish's teachings on the type of commitment it expects from them. This isn't necessarily a stewardship issue. Parishes that aren't heavily invested in stewardship might still expect their members to make some sort of financial or time commitment to the parish. But every parish that takes stewardship seriously should be clear about the level of stewardship commitment that it expects from its parishioners. Stewardship cannot be a casual undertaking.

This expectation generally takes the form of some variation of "first fruits." Recognizing God's generosity to us, we should make returning a portion of our time, talent, and treasure to further His work on earth our first priority, not simply what is left over after we've satisfied all of our other earthly commitments. For example, this might entail contributing our wage income from the first hour(s) that we work each week.

Tithing

In many stewardship parishes, this involves asking parishioners for a commitment to tithe. The Biblical teaching of tithing, of course, emphasizes contributing 10% of our resources. Very few parishes insist that all 10% go to the parish. Some, for example, use the formula of 8% to the parish and 2% to other causes. Others might ask for a commitment of 5% to the parish and 5% to other causes. Some pastors tell their parishioners that they can count their parochial school tuition as a part of their tithe. And, of course, there will always be some parishioners who will ask if the tithe should be based on pre-tax or post-tax income.

Actually, very few Catholics tithe. The data that supported *Why Catholics Don't Give* was based on a survey primarily of regular Mass attendees. A high percentage (75%) of that sample indicated that they attended Mass **at least** weekly; yet, when asked about tithing, only 4% indicated that they did. In the survey that supports this study, only 18% of parishes asked their parishioners to tithe.

Some parishioners, while reluctant to tithe, will commit themselves to contributing an annual percentage of their income that is something less than a tithe. As with tithing, though, very few Catholics do this. Of the primarily regular Mass attendees reported on in *Why Catholic Don't Give*, only 6% indicated that their contributions were based on their goal to donate a given percentage of their income. Thirty-five percent of the parishes that responded to the survey for this study encouraged their parishioners to contribute a given percentage of their income.

In the survey for this book, only 5% of the parishes encouraged their members to contribute a specific dollar amount (e.g., $20 per week, or $1,000 per year). But that was the most popular approach taken by the regular Mass attendees in the *Why Catholics Don't Give* survey, with 53% indicating that was how they determined the amount that they would contribute to the parish.

Perhaps of greatest concern is the number of parishes who make no recommendation at all about how much their parishioners should be contributing. Thirty-six percent of the parishes responding to the survey supporting this book either made no recommendation at all or told parishioners that they could contribute whatever they thought they could afford. It's no wonder, then, that 37% of the regular Mass attendees in the *Why Catholics Don't Give* study based their giving decision on how much

Parish Teachings on Parishioners' Level of Support Decisions

they thought they could afford each week. We all know how that goes. If parishioners feel they can give more that week, they will. But if their checkbook is a bit light that week, they will give less (or nothing). And all too often, if they miss Mass for some reason (out of town, sick, etc.) they are unlikely to make up that week's contribution. I know. That used to be me.

In all honesty, if I am permitted to preach a bit of heresy here, I'm not a big fan of preaching about tithing to Catholics. My hesitation is based on three factors:

- First, tithing advocates emphasize that it is Biblically based. Yes, it is, if your Bible ends with the Hebrew Scriptures. But Jesus emphasized stewardship, not tithing; about the only time Jesus even mentions tithing is when he is mocking the Pharisees.
- Second, tithing tends to be too much about money. Little is ever said about the other two components of stewardship, time and talent. But stewardship is like a three-legged stool. We need all three to be complete.
- Finally, tithing is simply not practical for the typical Catholic household currently contributing 1% of their income to their parish. I've been in forums where tithing is being preached, and I watched as parishioners' eyes glazed over at the mention of the expectation that they will now begin contributing 10% (or 8%, or even 5%) of their income. It is simply not practical to ask someone who is contributing 1% of their income to make that sort of jump.

So, what should a parish be teaching? I'm an advocate of incremental giving. I would tell the typical parishioner who is currently contributing 1% of their income to try to increase it to 1.5% next year. Maybe 2% the following year, followed by an increase to 2.5%, and so on. Isn't that just a backdoor approach to tithing? Sure, it is. But it is one that most Catholics can relate to, and one that they can comfortably hope to achieve. It is realistic.

Pledging

I'm not a big fan of tithing, but I *am* a big fan of pledging. It is imperative that we ask our parishioners to make a firm commitment to support their parish.

Unfortunately, pledging is not a popular concept with Catholics, who were raised in a Church that relied on the freewill offerings that were deposited in the offertory collection basket each week. Many view pledging as a Protestant concept. Others worry about what would happen if their circumstances change, and they are unable to meet their pledge. Some are even concerned about what the pastor will think of them when he sees the amount they have pledged. I've even heard parishioners fret that the pastor will provide them with a cut-rate funeral or wedding if they aren't generous pledgers.

I recall sitting in a focus group of Catholic laity when the issue of tithing came up. One woman was very vehemently opposed, stating, "How can you expect me to commit to making a specific contribution for a **whole year!**" It may sound intimidating; on the other hand, many of us don't hesitate to take out a car loan for four years, or assume a mortgage for a vacation home. We need to ask ourselves, "What do *we* own, and what owns *us?*"

For Catholics hesitant to pledge, a few simple measures can help make the idea more palatable. Some parishes use tear-off pledge sheets, with one side listing the amount of the pledge, and the other side listing the parishioner's name. During the offertory on Commitment Sunday, parishioners are invited to the foot of the altar, where there are two baskets. They place the portion of the pledge sheet that contains their identifying information in one basket, and the other portion showing the amount of the pledge in the other basket. There is no way to associate the two. This allows the parish finance council to have a good idea of what parish income will look like in the coming year. Knowing who has pledged, without necessarily knowing how much they have

Parish Teachings on Parishioners' Level of Support Decisions

pledged, makes it easier to communicate with individual parishioners to thank them for their pledge. At the same time, it also alerts pastors as to those who have pledged and those who haven't. Many pastors find this information to be valuable. A parishioner who chooses not to pledge may have issues that the pastor should know about so that he can address them in a pastoral manner.

Another approach used by some parishes is to invite parishioners to process to the foot of the altar on Commitment Sunday and drop their pledges in a basket. Then, the pastor starts a small fire and burns the pledge sheets. The message is that your pledge is between you and God.

Still other parishes ask their members to pledge time, talent, and treasure. Based on the notion of first fruits, they ask their parishioners to pledge their first hour's wage each week, one hour spent in time praying or meditating, and one hour in contributing talent. The talent hour need not occur each week. Some weeks parishioners might not contribute any, but other weeks they might contribute two or three hours.

Many parishes make it easier for their parishioners to pledge by establishing a system for electronic funds transfers. Many parishioners (especially younger ones) routinely make payments (car payment, mortgage, utility bills, etc.) this way. This common way of exchanging funds in the twenty-first century is a relatively simple process; the parish simply arranges with local banks to transfer funds from parishioners' accounts to the parish account on a designated day each month.

There is a concern on the part of some pastors that allowing electronic funds transfers will diminish the importance of the offertory at Mass. But the offertory has changed over the years. At one time people brought real goods (livestock, grain) for their offertory gift. At some point, there was a radical change to replacing these goods with currency. Later, checks began to supplant currency. Moving to a system of electronic funds transfers is a natural progression.

To serve this need, many offering-envelope producers such as Our Sunday Visitor print envelopes with a box on the front that states that the contribution has been made electronically. So, at the offertory, parishioners deposit their envelopes. Some contain cash, some checks, and some are empty but have the box checked indicating that the contribution has been made electronically.

However, one danger with pledging — regardless of the form it takes — is that it can be disassociated from stewardship. Parishioners might view their pledge merely as necessary to meet the budget; they give to a need, rather than develop a need to give. Pastors need to preach on stewardship to ensure that parishioners don't base their pledge merely on their satisfaction with the parish's programs.

Survey Findings

Encouraging parishioners to make a commitment to support their parish, whether it is through tithing, pledging, or some other means, is one strategy generally believed to be effective. But is it? In Table 8.1, we see that the answer is a qualified "Yes."

Encouraging parishioners to tithe their income has a substantial impact on parishioners' treasure contributions. As we have noted, only about one-sixth of the parishes in this survey promoted tithing. But those that did received an average of 27% larger per-household financial contributions. Unfortunately, this generosity did not spill over to other contributions, such as volunteer time or time spent in spiritual practices. Tithing treasure was associated with a significantly larger parish outreach effort.

Somewhat inexplicably, parishes that requested their parishioners to consider proportional giving (but not at the level of a tithe) did not receive larger financial contributions, but did enjoy moderately greater volunteer time and were more engaged in outreach.

The most successful approach was to ask parishioners to pledge. Parishes that encouraged pledging of treasure received

Parish Teachings on Parishioners' Level of Support Decisions

TABLE 8.1
Parish Teachings on Giving

Parish Teaching	Treasure	Volunteer Time	Spiritual Time	Outreach Time
TREASURE				
Tithe Treasure (18%)	1.27	*	*	1.20
Proportion of Income (35%)	*	1.08	*	1.12
PLEDGING				
Pledge Treasure (54%)	1.16	1.09	*	1.17
Pledge Time (43%)	1.13	1.14	*	1.15
Pledge Talent (46%)	1.12	1.15	*	1.12
PLEDGE FOLLOW-UP				
Send Pledge Thank-you (75%)	*	1.13	*	1.21
Send Pledge Reminder (44%)	1.38	*	1.18	1.27

significantly larger contributions of treasure, volunteer time, and outreach activities. **The same was true for parishes that practiced pledging of time and talent.** Pledging time, talent, and treasure resulted in significantly larger contributions of all three.

The increase in treasure in all three of these cases was not as great as it was for tithing, but pledging had a broader impact on parish stewardship outcomes than did tithing.

Parishes that promote pledging need to consider whether or not they want to identify the households making pledges. Though many Catholics are reluctant to have anyone in the parish house have specific information on their pledge, those parishes that do have some information are in a position to thank those who have pledged and send out periodic reminders about the status of their pledge. In the former case, it is not necessary that the pledged amount be known.

In Table 8.1, we see that 75% of the parishes that pledged sent out a thank-you, and 44% sent reminders. Sending a thank-you to those who had pledged was only effective in generating significantly more volunteer contributions and outreach effort. Sending reminders resulted in a large increase in treasure contributions — 38% greater than in the average for the sample. This was an even greater impact on treasure than tithing! Somewhat surprisingly, reminders were also associated with significantly more time spent in spiritual practices and parish outreach effort. So, while parishioners might be reluctant to have someone in the parish know about and keep track of their pledge amount, the ability to use this information and issue reminders can be a very effective stewardship tool.

Summary

For stewardship to be fully effective, we need parishioners to make a commitment to the parish concerning their contributions of time, talent, and treasure. Unfortunately, Catholics are not accustomed to making stewardship commitments to their parish. Our evangelical Protestant friends generally accept their responsibility to tithe, and mainline Protestants are comfortable with pledging, but Catholics tend not to be comfortable with either approach. It requires a cultural change among Catholic parishioners to persuade them to make a similar commitment.

The empirical results reported in this chapter come down heavily in favor of pledging over tithing as an effective strategy for generating a stewardship commitment on the part of Catholics — although the two are not mutually exclusive. Tithing is extremely effective at increasing the treasure component of stewardship; pledging is found to be successful at increasing volunteer hours as well as treasure. This is true whether parishioners are asked to pledge time, talent, or treasure.

Whatever approach a parish chooses, it is clear that any attempt to encourage a commitment on the part of parishioners to support the parish is superior to the approach taken by far too many of our parishioners today: "I'll decide weekly how much I can afford to contribute."

REFERENCE

Zech, Charles E. *Why Catholics Don't Give . . . And What Can Be Done About It* (Updated). Huntington, IN: Our Sunday Visitor, 2006.

Chapter Nine

PARISH WELCOMING AND COMMUNITY-BUILDING ACTIVITIES

People give to people. All professional fundraisers are aware of this basic motivation. We might be able to raise funds for a specific project: say, the roof blew off the school, or the boiler in the church broke down. But generally, people are most generous when they can identify with the recipient of their generosity. For proof, just ask yourself which is a more effective approach to raising money for missions — having the pastor announce at Mass that next Sunday there will be a special collection for the missions, or having a missionary speak at Mass and tell stories about life in the mission fields, with specific examples of the situations that people find themselves in and how they could be helped by a donation? The answer is pretty obvious.

People give to people. This is even more apparent when the people are close to them, such as their fellow parishioners. Then the donor can see and feel the good that results from the donation firsthand, and maybe even experience it themselves. It is imperative, then, that the parish nurture a sense of community among its parishioners. Parishioners who feel a sense of community with their fellow parishioners can be expected to be more generous in their contributions of time, talent, and treasure.

Being a welcoming parish and engaging in community-building activities are not unique to stewardship parishes. Even parishes unconcerned with stewardship would presumably recognize the importance of welcoming and community-building, but it is one of the preconditions to becoming a stewardship parish. If a parish is not viewed as welcoming, if parishioners don't feel a sense of community, the parish should not bother with stewardship; it won't take hold. So, before a parish begins to introduce stewardship, it needs to ask itself about the state of community in the parish. If there are rifts (school parents vs. religious education parents, veteran parishioners vs. new parishioners, one ethnic group vs. another, etc.), the parish must work to heal them before introducing stewardship. Of course, being a welcoming place and building community are continuous. A parish can never sit back and say to itself, "Well, we've built a sense of community, so there is no need to work on that anymore."

In "Stewardship and Development in Catholic Dioceses and Parishes: A Resource Manual," the U.S. Catholic Bishops recognized the importance of parish welcoming and community-building activities:

> Communities known for the vitality of their faith and for the quality of their service to people in need invariably inspire others to participate in their ministries and to be generous in their financial support. With this in mind, parishes and dioceses that seek to promote gifts of time, talent, and treasure to support the mission and ministries of the Church should first demonstrate that they are welcoming communities with a commitment to preaching the Gospel and serving the needs of others.

This sense of community starts with the parish promoting a welcoming environment to new parishioners, and extends to other activities designed to cultivate a sense of community among all parishioners. This can be a real challenge in a Catholic parish, where it is not unusual to have 3,000 or more households. But the parish needs to do everything it can to develop community — to behave as though it were a small, tight-knit group.

Parish Welcoming and Community-Building Activities

We saw in Chapter Three that parishes that have more than 1,750 households (medium-sized in today's Church) actually receive significantly **lower** contributions of treasure, and we noted the impact of the tendency of parishioners to "free-ride." This tendency can be mitigated by activities intended to build a sense of parish community.

The researchers cited in Chapter Two found that welcoming and community-building activities were critical to the success of the parishes that they visited. For example, in *Called to Be Stewards: Bringing New Life to Catholic Parishes*, Patrick McNamara observed that community-building activities, such as coffee-and-donut receptions between Masses or parish picnics, provide an opportunity for parishioners to break away from their cliques and mingle with those they might not otherwise encounter. He cited the role of small faith communities as critical to the successful stewardship that he found in one of the parishes that he visited, Corpus Christi Parish in Fremont, California.

Another parish that McNamara visited, the Church of St. John the Baptist in Covington, Washington, held quarterly "Pizza with the Pastor" events, where new parishioners could join the pastor and staff in an informal setting to learn more about the parish. That same parish held welcome gatherings every six weeks, where parishioners participated in a faith-sharing exercise in which they shared significant points in their faith journey.

You might recall that Paul Wilkes (*Excellent Catholic Parishes: The Guide to Best Places and Practices*) learned from Msgr. McGread, of St. Francis of Assisi Parish in Wichita, that successful stewardship is built upon three legs: prayer, service, and **hospitality**. Justin Clement (*Stewardship: A Parish Handbook*) expands on that theme by remarking that when a parish is hospitable, it is not just a place where people go but a place where they **want** to be. He emphasizes that hospitality is the responsibility of every parishioner, not just those who might have been designated as "greeters" or "hospitality ministers."

BEST PRACTICES IN PARISH STEWARDSHIP

As our parishes get larger — in the face of declining numbers of vocations and the need to merge and otherwise reconfigure parishes — it becomes critical that they take advantage of every opportunity available to build community, to make the parish seem small and welcoming.

I recall visiting a priest who was very much an advocate of stewardship. He had recently been transferred to serve as pastor in a different parish. I asked him how it was going, especially with respect to stewardship. He responded that it was going to be a slow process, but he knew the importance of being patient in introducing stewardship — but then, he told me that the first thing he had done was cancel the parish's annual festival. "Raising money through a festival," he remarked, "is not stewardship."

At the time I nodded in agreement, but later, I reconsidered. What a counterproductive idea! What better way to build community than with a parish festival — where parishioners of all ages, socioeconomic standings, and commitment levels can mingle and work together?

Later, at an ICSC conference, I had lunch with some parishioners from a fairly large parish in Florida. They began telling me about their parish festival, which had more than 1,000 parishioners involved. (Presumably, some parishioners may have worked in a booth for an hour, or helped clean up, or the like.) When I asked them whether the festival had raised any money, they responded, "Yes, it raised $90,000. **But we had more than 1,000 parishioners involved!**" Now, what parish, no matter what its size, couldn't use $90,000? But to them, the important outcome was parishioner involvement and community building. They seemingly had it right.

It sounds logical that welcoming and community-building activities should be important to every parish, whether it is emphasizing stewardship or not. But do they lead to better stewardship outcomes? Our findings are in Table 9.1.

TABLE 9.1
Impact of Welcoming/Community-Building Activities

	Treasure	Volunteer Time	Spiritual Time	Outreach Time
WELCOMING ACTIVITY (PERCENTAGE UTILIZING)				
Greeters at Mass (75%)	1.05	1.05	1.05	1.07
Encouraging Parishioners to Be Welcoming toward Strangers (34%)	*	1.11	1.17	1.15
Welcoming Table Outside Mass (17%)	*	*	1.20	1.21
Welcome Wagon — Visit New Parishioners (16%)	*	1.18	*	*
New Members Reception (41%)	1.13	1.09	*	1.26
Four or More Welcoming Activities (Average 1.8)	**1.38**	**1.23**	**1.26**	**1.41**
COMMUNITY-BUILDING ACTIVITY				
Coffee/Donuts after Mass (73%)	1.06	1.04	*	1.07
Parish Picnic (55%)	1.08	1.07	1.07	1.11
Parish Festival (51%)	*	*	*	*
Bingo (11%)	*	*	*	*
Boy/Girl Scouts (46%)	1.07	*	*	1.15
Parish-Sponsored Sports Programs (31%)	1.13	*	*	1.18
Potluck Dinners (47%)	1.09	1.13	1.13	1.09
Four or More Community-Building Activities (Average 3.8)	**1.10**	**1.12**	*	**1.19**

Welcoming Activities

We asked our respondents about five specific welcoming activities. In addition, we allowed them to indicate others if they desired. The average number of welcoming activities utilized by the parishes in our sample was 1.8.

Based on its ability to impact all four stewardship outcome measures, assigning "greeters" or "hospitality ministers" to each Mass is the most effective welcoming activity. Three-fourths of the parishes in our sample utilized greeters. Although only about a third of the parishes in our sample did so, encouraging parishioners to be welcoming was effective at increasing all of the stewardship outcomes except for treasure. In fact, based on the magnitude of the coefficients, encouraging parishioners to be welcoming has a greater impact on volunteer time, spiritual time, and outreach time than does employing greeters.

Another relatively successful welcoming activity was holding a new members' reception, sponsored by 41% of the parishes in the sample. These were associated with significant increases in treasure, volunteer time, and outreach time.

Other welcoming activities, such as setting up a welcoming table outside of each Mass or visiting each newly registered parishioner with a "Welcome Wagon"-type packet, were each used by only about a sixth of the parishes in the sample. They varied in their impact on stewardship outcomes. The former had a significant effect on both spiritual time and outreach time, and the latter significantly impacted volunteer time.

The real payoff to welcoming activities comes when they are used in combination. Parishes that engaged in four or more welcoming activities experienced significantly larger amounts of each of the four stewardship outcomes. In fact, for each stewardship outcome, the index associated with using four or more welcoming activities was greater than it had been for any single welcoming activity.

Community-Building Activities

We asked our sample about their offering of seven different community-building activities, along with any others that they might wish to include. As Table 9.1 indicates, two of them — sponsoring a parish picnic and holding potluck dinners — were associated with significantly larger stewardship outcomes in all four categories. Each was sponsored by about half of the parishes in the sample. Two others had no significant impact on any of the stewardship outcomes: holding a parish festival (contrary to my belief) and sponsoring bingo (11% of the parishes in the sample still sponsored bingo).

A relatively successful community-building activity, and one that was most frequently used by parishes (about three-fourths) in our sample, was holding coffee/donut receptions between Masses. This activity was associated with significantly higher levels of parish treasure, volunteer hours, and outreach efforts.

All of these activities are typically open to the entire parish, and all would accomplish the goal as described by Patrick McNamara: providing parishioners the opportunity to mingle with other parishioners with whom they might not otherwise associate.

We also asked about two activities aimed at the youth of the parish (and, by extension, their parents). One was scouts, the other parish-sponsored sports programs. Both were associated with significantly larger amounts of treasure and parish outreach. I had anticipated that since both types of programs rely extensively on parent volunteers, they would also have a significant impact on parish volunteer hours, but this didn't prove to be the case.

As with many of the activities that we've considered thus far, the total number of community-building activities is, in many respects, more important than any single activity. Parishes that offered four or more community-building activities received significantly greater contributions in three stewardship areas: treasure, volunteer time, and outreach.

Summary

Every parish, whether it has a stewardship motivation or not, should be concerned that it is perceived as a welcoming place where parishioners want to be, and where they enjoy a sense of community. However, being a welcoming place and providing a sense of community, in and of themselves, are not sufficient conditions for a parish to experience increased stewardship in its parishioners. But unless parishioners feel welcome and feel a sense of community, the stewardship message will likely fail to get through to them.

Additionally, here's a case where the whole is greater than its individual parts. Parishes that sponsored four or more welcoming activities not only enjoyed significantly greater levels of each stewardship outcome, but based on the coefficients, the impact on each outcome was larger than for any single welcoming activity. Likewise, those parishes that engaged in four or more community-building activities received significantly larger contributions of treasure, volunteer time, and outreach effort.

REFERENCES

Clements, C. Justin. *Stewardship: A Parish Handbook*. Ligouri, MO: Ligouri Press, 2000.

McNamara, Patrick H. *Called to Be Stewards: Bringing New Life to Catholic Parishes*. Collegeville, MN: The Liturgical Press, 2003.

"Stewardship and Development in Catholic Dioceses and Parishes: A Resource Manual." In *Stewardship: A Disciple's Response*, Tenth Anniversary Edition. Washington, DC: USCCB, 2002.

Wilkes, Paul. *Excellent Catholic Parishes: The Guide to Best Places and Practices.* New York: Paulist Press, 2001.

Chapter Ten

COMMUNICATIONS ON STEWARDSHIP

Every parish should be concerned with communicating with its parishioners. If we want parishioners to take an active interest in the parish, we need to keep them informed on parish activities. This is true even for parishes not striving to be stewardship parishes, but is especially critical for those that are.

The U.S. Catholic Bishops recognized the importance of communication in "Stewardship and Development in Catholic Dioceses and Parishes: A Resource Manual":

> Given the competition that exists today for people's time and attention, parishes and dioceses that wish to be successful in stewardship and development must pay careful attention to the effectiveness of their communications. Especially since most dioceses and parishes are working with very limited communications budgets, the choices that are made about how to most effectively "tell our story" or "make our case" can be crucial to success.

Parishes have a variety of means to communicate with parishioners. Historically, the most common have been through announcements from the pulpit and the weekly parish bulletin. But these reach only those parishioners present on a given Sunday. In recent years, recognizing the decline in Sunday Mass attendance, some parishes have begun mailing reports directly to parishioners' homes. Many parishes have established a parish newsletter that contains an assortment of news items about recent and future events in the parish. Of course, with home computer ownership so common, it is critical that every parish have its own Web site.

These and other communication tools are helpful in disseminating announcements, posting of schedules, and other routine parish activities. They can also be a valuable tool in promoting stewardship in the parish. This chapter considers two ways in which these communication tools can be essential stewardship tools: first, to focus attention on the meaning of stewardship and its importance in parishioners' lives; and second, to spotlight and celebrate examples of good stewardship, especially in the contribution of time and talent, by individual parishioners or parish groups.

Communications to Focus Attention on Stewardship

As noted earlier, one of the most effective ways of focusing parishioners' attention on stewardship is through the homily. Opportunities to connect the Sunday readings to a stewardship homily abound. But even the most die-hard stewardship advocate would recognize that preaching about stewardship every (or nearly every) Sunday would quickly reach the point of diminishing returns. That is why it is so important to use other vehicles to communicate about stewardship on a regular basis.

Our focus groups had some varied experiences on the most effective stewardship communication tools:

- "Sending out stuff in the parents' packet that the school sends home we think has been pretty effective."
- "We try to include a message about stewardship in every communication — the weekly bulletin, mailings that probably hit parish households (for various things) monthly, etc."
- "Our weekly bulletin has both an adult and a youth stewardship corner. We send out a monthly newsletter with

two or three stewardship articles. Stewardship banners are displayed regularly."
- "Monthly bulletin inserts from the Archdiocese have been useful. We do a flyer every six months about stewardship. We also have bulletin reflections on what stewardship of time means (personal testimony by parishioners)."
- "We question the effectiveness of bulletin inserts because there is so much stuff in the bulletin nowadays."
- "We use a stewardship thought each week in the bulletin, but it doesn't do much without having more said from the pulpit."
- "We communicate with parishioners on stewardship in a quarterly parish newsletter. We are expanding communication via our Web site, but it is hard to do without a professional to update the Web site."
- "We have tried to get more on stewardship on our Web site, but it never seems to get anywhere."
- "Spending money on inserts and brochures has not improved our people's understanding of stewardship."
- "Our parish stewardship logo appears on all mailings."
- "We have started a stewardship library in the vestibule, though we need to make it 'present' to more people, like by putting the racks on wheels and 'forcing' people to walk by them."
- "The stewardship prayer is used as the closing prayer for intercessions."

There are any number of ways to communicate about the meaning of stewardship with parishioners. We asked our sample about seven specific ones. They were given the opportunity to add to our list if they so desired. Our findings are shown in the top portion of Table 10.1.

Nearly every parish in our sample used the parish bulletin at one point or another to communicate about the meaning of

TABLE 10.1
Parish Communications on Stewardship

	Treasure	Volunteer Time	Spiritual Time	Outreach Time
COMMUNICATION TO FOCUS ATTENTION ON STEWARDSHIP				
Pulpit Announcements (70%)	1.04	1.05	*	1.08
Parish Bulletin (93%)	*	*	*	1.03
Parish Newsletter (32%)	1.23	1.21	1.12	1.23
Ministry Booklet (42%)	1.09	1.15	*	1.23
Stewardship Literature Available (47%)	1.08	1.11	*	1.16
Prayers of the Faithful (56%)	1.08	1.07	*	1.14
Parish Web Site (41%)	1.13	1.16	*	1.25
Five or More Communications Media (Average 4.0)	**1.14**	**1.19**	**1.10**	**1.30**
COMMUNICATION TO SPOTLIGHT CONTRIBUTIONS OF TIME AND TALENT				
Parish Bulletin (57%)	*	1.07	*	1.08
Parish Web Site (14%)	*	1.24	1.21	1.22
Mailed Directly to Parishioners (24%)	*	1.13	1.18	1.19
Presented at Weekend Masses (18%)	*	*	*	1.13
Parish Newsletter (16%)	1.26	1.23	1.19	1.27
Three or More Report Media (Average 1.4)	**1.21**	**1.21**	**1.17**	**1.31**

stewardship with parishioners. Likewise, nearly all utilized pulpit announcements. But the most effective communications tool, at least in terms of influencing all four stewardship outcome measures, was the use of a parish newsletter. Only about a third of the parishes in our sample employed a parish newsletter for this purpose, but those who did found it to be very effective.

Most of the other communications tools were associated with significantly greater levels of treasure, volunteer time, and parish outreach effort. The one exception was the parish bulletin. But this could be a statistical quirk; since nearly every parish used it for this purpose, it is difficult to ascertain whether it is an effective tool or not.

Somewhat surprisingly, the parish Web site was the second-least-used stewardship communications tool by the parishes in our sample. Earlier, we had noted the differences in attitudes towards the institutional Church among the generational cohorts, and the difficulties in attracting the younger members of our parish. Clearly, this cohort is the most comfortable with technology and the group most likely to be attracted to information contained on a parish Web site. Parishes need to rethink their attitudes toward this underutilized instrument of evangelization.

One of the lessons to be learned from Table 10.1 is that, once again, a combination of stewardship activities is most effective. The average number of media used by parishes in our sample to communicate with parishioners on the meaning of stewardship and its importance in their lives was four. But those parishes that utilized five or more experienced significantly larger amounts of all four of our stewardship outcomes.

Communications to Spotlight Contributions of Time and Talent

It is generally believed that one of the most effective ways to communicate stewardship, especially the time and talent components, is to spotlight examples of successful stewardship in the parish. This could take the form of publicizing good stewardship by either individual parishioners or parish groups. Just as lay witness talks by fellow parishioners can serve to inspire parishioners, so too, communicating examples of good stewardship can serve to convince parishioners that their own contributions of their time and talent can make a difference. At the same time, publicly acknowledging the successes of individual parishioners or parish groups can motivate them to continue in their ministry.

Communicating on parishioner time and talent accomplishments is important for a variety of reasons, not the least of which is to remind parishioners that stewardship is not just a fundraising gimmick; that it is about more than just treasure. In fact, this is so important that many stewardship councils have a communications subcommittee to carry out this task.

Based on the comments by the members of our focus groups, spotlighting individual contributions of time and talent stewardship is a popular approach. Some representative comments were:

- "Dedicating a full page of the bulletin to stewardship seems to have educated people. We highlight one volunteer per week. Our bulletin features a column on everyday stewards."
- "The best thing that we do to teach stewardship is to highlight a different ministry each week. This helps people understand that stewardship is not just about money."
- "We devote one page to stewardship in every bulletin. It is used to offer gratitude to those in the parish who are stewardship examples, as well as teach some small element of stewardship."

In our survey, we asked respondents about their use of five different methods of communicating to the entire parish about individual examples of parishioner contributions of time and talent. They were given the opportunity to add others to the list. Our findings are found in the lower half of Table 10.1.

More than half of the parishes used the parish bulletin for this purpose. But only a small minority of parishes used each of the other available media to communicate individual examples of good stewardship.

As might be expected, because we are concerned here only with communicating successful stories of time and talent contributions, the treasure component of stewardship tended not to be affected by these activities. The notable exception was, once again, the parish newsletter. All four of our stewardship outcome mea-sures were significantly affected when parishes used their newsletter to publicize individual accomplishments in time and talent stewardship.

Two methods of communication, the parish Web site and mailing reports directly to parishioners, significantly impacted three stewardship measures, but as noted, were used by a small minority of parishes (only 14% used their Web site for this purpose).

Once again, though, using a combination of communications media was found to be effective. The average number of media used to communicate individual accomplishments of time and talent stewardship by the parishes in our sample was 1.4. But those parishes that employed three or more received significantly larger contributions of all four measures of our stewardship outcomes.

Summary

Communication is an important function for all parishes. If we want parishioners to feel a commitment to the parish, we need to communicate with them about past and future events.

As important as communication is in general, it is even more critical for stewardship parishes. As the U.S. Catholic bishops have observed, a great deal of competition exists today for people's time and attention. We need to regularly remind our parishioners of the meaning of stewardship and its importance in their lives and to spotlight and celebrate examples of good stewardship by individual parishioners or parish groups.

Our survey asked about the media used for both of these communications functions. We found parish newsletters to be the most effective in terms of impacting all four stewardship outcome measures. Consistent with our findings in previous chapters, the real payoff comes when parishes utilize more than one communications vehicle.

Somewhat discouraging was the low level at which parish Web sites were used to communicate about stewardship. In an era when the Church is finding it difficult, for whatever reason, to connect with young adults, it is astounding that more parishes don't recognize the potential payoff from the use of technology. This is how young adults communicate. Parishes need to catch up, not only with regards to stewardship, but with regards to the parish's entire mission.

REFERENCE

U.S. Conference of Catholic Bishops. "Stewardship and Development in Catholic Dioceses and Parishes: A Resource Manual," in *Stewardship: A Disciple's Response*, Tenth Anniversary Edition. Washington, DC: USCCB, 2002.

Chapter Eleven

FINANCIAL ACCOUNTABILITY AND TRANSPARENCY

We began our analysis of parish stewardship practices by talking about the importance of parish leadership. We conclude on that same theme.

All of the researchers cited — Justin Clements, Daniel Conway, Patrick McNamara, Paul Wilkes, etc. — have emphasized the importance of the pastor's support in order for stewardship to thrive in a parish. But it is not enough for the pastor to "talk the talk." He must also "walk the walk." Parishioners take their stewardship cues from the example set by the parish house.

Stewardship in the Parish House

Let me provide three examples.

I know of a pastor who thought it was important to beautify the parish church by purchasing some new doors. Without any consultation with the lay leadership bodies in the parish, he went ahead and bought new doors with a price tag of $38,000. One parishioner confronted the pastor and pointed out that (based on the 1% of income contributed to the Church cited earlier in this book) $38,000 was more than most parishioners would contribute to their parish in their lifetime. The pastor had, in effect, taken a parishioner's lifetime contributions, and rather than use them for the myriad of high-priority items needed in the parish, he used them to buy doors. And he hadn't consulted with anyone. Can he really expect parishioners to increase their financial contributions when this is how the funds will be spent? What credibility does this pastor have when he preaches on stewardship?

In another case, a pastor who was expanding the parish school ran into a cost overrun. Parishioners recognize that these things happen. The pastor announced the cost overrun ($49,000) at Sunday Mass. The next week, he announced that a relatively new parishioner (he had been a member of the parish for only a month) had stepped forward and written a check for $49,000. The next month, the pastor appointed the parishioner to a seat on the parish pastoral council, even though the council's bylaws specified a three-year parish membership to be eligible to sit on the council. Parishioners concluded that the pastor had "sold" that pastoral council seat.

Finally, there is the case of a priest who pastored a wealthy suburban parish located near one of the poorest communities in the United States. Even though surrounding parishes tended to tithe their collections revenue and use the money for outreach to this poverty-stricken community, this particular parish budgeted nothing for outreach programs. In the parish annual report, the pastor listed the Cathedraticum (the tax on parish collections sent to the diocese) as the parish's charitable contribution. It was pointed out to this pastor that a tax can't really be considered a charitable contribution. If it was, virtually every parishioner in that parish would be considered to be tithing, since the parish paid more than 10% of their income in taxes. In any event, it was argued, it was scandalous that this wealthy parish failed to contribute any of its collections revenue to support those in need. The pastor, however, was unmoved. He continued to list the Cathedraticum as parish charity, while budgeting nothing from regular parish collections for outreach.

I frequently use examples like these when making public presentations on stewardship. Afterwards, I'm typically swarmed by attendees who say something like, "You think that was bad. Wait until I tell you what **my** pastor did. . . !" Let's be very clear. Good

Financial Accountability and Transparency

stewardship starts in the parish house. If we want our parishioners to take stewardship seriously, if we really hope to achieve a conversion of minds and hearts, it is critical that the parish exhibit good stewardship in the way it spends its parishioners' contributions. Otherwise, what credibility does a pastor have when he preaches on stewardship?

But appropriate expenditures on the part of the parish are only part of the pastor's stewardship responsibility. He must also ensure that the parish is not the victim of fraud, and that the parish is transparent and accountable to parishioners in all of its financial dealings.

Recently, along with my Villanova colleague, Dr. Robert West, I conducted a study of diocesan financial practices. Among our findings was that 85% of U.S. dioceses had experienced some embezzlement within the last five years. If one believes the headlines, these embezzlements typically take place at the parish level, due to poor internal financial controls. Both priests and lay staff have been convicted of fraud. Among the common internal financial control abuses that occur at the parish level that could lead to financial fraud and embezzlements are:

- Allowing the same person (or group of persons) to count the Sunday collection every week
- Allowing the same person who deposits parish funds to also be responsible for reconciling the parish checkbook
- Requiring only one signature on checks written for large amounts
- Maintaining numerous parish checking accounts
- Failing to conduct financial audits on a regular (preferably an annual) basis

The problem is that we tend to be too trusting. No one would think that a priest or lay staff member would embezzle Church funds, so we fail to put into place the types of internal financial controls that are common in the private sector.

BEST PRACTICES IN PARISH STEWARDSHIP

Related to effective internal financial controls are issues of financial accountability and transparency. At a minimum, parishioners need to be kept informed of the parish's financial condition through regular, easily accessible, and understandable reports and updates. Preferably, parishioners would be brought into the financial decision-making process. This could be accomplished by holding open parish hearings as the annual parish budget is being formulated, presenting a preliminary draft to parishioners and establishing a mechanism for them to provide input, and making parish finance council members available to answer questions about the parish budget and other parish financial matters.

In their document, "Stewardship and Development in Catholic Dioceses and Parishes: A Resource Manual," the U.S. Catholic bishops address the issue of accountability:

> Success in the stewardship and development efforts of a parish or diocese requires a visible commitment to accountability. This commitment includes accountability for the full range of parish or diocesan activities—from the way decisions are made and carried out by diocesan or parish personnel to the way money is collected, managed, and used. **Indeed, accountability is fundamental to good stewardship** . . . A visible commitment to accountability will be reflected in the leadership styles and attitudes of the bishop, pastor, and all who have responsibilities for the human, physical, and financial resources of the diocese or parish. **Like personal witness, a commitment to accountability is essential to building a solid foundation for a diocesan or parish stewardship program** (emphases added).

The bishops go on to specify the importance of preparing annual reports that promote the understanding of the uses of the parish's or diocese's resources in fulfilling their mission.

Financial Accountability and Transparency

In a series of national surveys that I conducted in partnership with FADICA (Foundations and Donors Interested in Catholic Activities), we found that, in general, parishioners tend to believe that the Church is not as accountable and transparent as they would like. About two-thirds thought that the Church needs to be more accountable in its finances. Fewer than half felt that they had an adequate understanding of how their contributions are used. About two-thirds believed that both parishes and dioceses should be subject to an annual independent audit, and approximately 80% approved of open forums to discuss parish finances.

The National Leadership Roundtable on Church Management, headquartered in Washington, DC, has issued a pamphlet titled *A Parishioner's Guide to Understanding Parish Finances*. Included in the pamphlet is a section listing questions that parishioners should be asking their parish leadership about parish finances. Among the items are:

- Does my parish release statistics from prior years for comparison and to identify trends?
- Does my parish release regular budget updates showing actual revenues and expenditures in comparison to the approved budget?
- Does my parish have policies on conflicts of interest?
- Is there a regularly scheduled audit of the parish by an independent auditor to assess the parish's financial controls and health, with the results made public to parishioners?
- Are there oversight policies for receipt/handling and disbursement of parish funds handled by individuals?

It is important to emphasize that canon law reserves the final decision on all parish matters, including parish finances, to the pastor. The vast majority of parishioners are comfortable with this arrangement. They just want a consultative process that provides the opportunity for input on important parish decisions, such as the parish budget, and keeps them informed through accountable and transparent financial policies.

Approaches to Financial Accountability and Transparency

We asked our sample about their use of an assortment of approaches to being financially accountable and transparent. The results can be found in Table 11.1.

One approach is to hold open hearings to discuss parish finances and the parish budget. As indicated previously, the FADICA study on donor attitudes revealed that 80% of regular Mass-attending Catholics approved of this approach. But only 14% of the parishes in our sample indicated that they held these open forums. As might be expected, this approach was very effective in generating significantly greater contributions of treasure. It was also associated with higher levels of outreach activity. But it did not have a significant impact on either volunteer time or spiritual activities.

Most of the parishes (79%) indicated that that they made financial reports available through the weekly bulletin. This could take many forms, ranging from information on the average parish envelope contribution (a good idea, since most of us don't want to be considered "below average"), to a report on the previous week's collection (often compared to that same week from a year earlier), to general information regarding the current state of the budget — are revenues running ahead of or behind expenditures? Of course, it could also include a full financial report distributed as an insert to the Sunday bulletin. In any event, this proved to be a relatively weak approach, only modestly impacting contributions of treasure and having no effect on any of the other stewardship measures.

We had earlier emphasized how important it is that parishes develop Web sites and learn to communicate through them effectively. This is especially true if we want to reach younger

TABLE 11.1
Financial Accountability

REPORT METHOD	Treasure	Volunteer Time	Spiritual Time	Outreach Time
Open Parish Forum to Discuss Parish Finances/Budget (14%)	1.29	*	*	1.21
Reports in Weekly Bulletin (79%)	1.04	*	*	*
Reports Posted on Parish Web Site (18%)	*	*	*	1.15
Reports Mailed Directly to Parishioners (42%)	*	*	*	1.14
Reports Presented at Weekend Masses (31%)	*	*	*	*
Reports Included in Regular Parish Newsletter (19%)	1.20	1.22	1.17	1.19
Four or More Report Methods (Average 2.1)	**1.23**	**1.16**	*	**1.20**

Note: 2% of the parishes in the sample did not issue any parish financial reports cohorts. Unfortunately, only 18% of the parishes in our sample made financial reports available on their Web site. As a result, this, too, was an ineffective approach, associated only with more outreach activities.

Many (42%) of the parishes in our sample mailed financial reports directly to parishioners' homes. This is a good idea in that it ensures that everyone in the parish — including those who, for whatever reason, are infrequent Mass attendees and those who would be unlikely to attend an open forum or check the parish Web site — has the opportunity to be made aware of parish finances. In fact, it is puzzling that more parishes don't utilize this approach. On the other hand, like posting information on Web sites, mailing reports directly to the home impacted only the outreach measure.

Almost a third of the parishes communicated their finances at weekend Masses. This frequently takes the form of the pastor or (preferably) a member of the parish finance council presenting a brief report on the parish's annual budget. It is probably not a good idea to give the treasure component of stewardship this kind of attention at Mass unless the other components of stewardship receive a similar amount of attention. It could send the message that, in the end, all the parish cares about is money, and stewardship is only a fundraising scheme. In any event, this approach was unsuccessful at increasing any of our stewardship outcome mea-sures.

We saw earlier that one of the most successful tools for communicating about time and talent was the parish newsletter. The same can be said for using the newsletter as a means of being financially accountable and transparent. Reporting on the parish budget and finances through a parish newsletter significantly increased all four stewardship outcome measures, even though only 19% of the parishes in our sample used that approach. Not only does the parish newsletter provide the opportunity to present parishioners with a more complete budget and financial report than bulletin inserts or reports at Mass; it is more likely to be read than a mailing that is solely a financial report or a report posted on the parish Web site.

Finally, as with nearly every other stewardship activity that we've studied, using multiple approaches was effective. Whereas the average parish in our sample used 2.1 methods to inform parishioners about its finances, those that utilized four or more enjoyed significantly greater contributions of treasure, volunteer time, and outreach activity.

Summary

Parishioners who are serious about their stewardship know that there are plenty of ways that they can carry it out. Giving to the parish is only one way. Contributions to second collections, sister parishes, Catholic Charities, and even some secular causes can be outlets for good stewardship. If a parish wants to receive its fair share of parishioners' contributions of time, talent, and treasure, it must assure them that these contributions will be used wisely and will not be subject to fraud — and that they will be made aware of how their funds are used through the parish's transparency and accountability.

We found that the most effective approach for the parish to demonstrate accountability and transparency is to include financial and budgetary reports in a newsletter sent to all parish households. This assures that all parishioners at least have the opportunity to become aware of the parish's financial situation. Holding open hearings on the parish budget was also found to be effective in increasing the treasure component of stewardship. None of the other approaches to parish financial accountability and transparency were found to be particularly effective by themselves — but when used in combination (four or more), they had a significantly positive effect on treasure, volunteer time, and parish outreach efforts.

REFERENCES

Catholic Donor Attitude Survey. Washington, DC: FADICA, 2005.

A Parishioner's Guide to Understanding Parish Finances. Washington, DC: National Leadership Roundtable on Church Management, 2007.

U.S. Conference of Catholic Bishops. "Stewardship and Development in Catholic Dioceses and Parishes: A Resource Manual," in *Stewardship: A Disciple's Response*, Tenth Anniversary Edition. Washington, DC: USCCB, 2002.

West, Robert, and Charles Zech. "Internal Financial Controls in the U.S. Catholic Church." *Journal of Forensic Accounting*, Vol. 9, No. 1 (June 2008), pp. 129-55. Flourtown, PA: R.T. Edwards, 2008.

Chapter Twelve

EIGHT THINGS THAT PARISHES CAN DO TO ADVANCE STEWARDSHIP

There are a variety of activities that parishes can engage in as they attempt to instill a sense of stewardship in their parishioners. We considered a number of them in this book. All have their advocates who can cite anecdotal evidence concerning their effectiveness. But which ones really work? What are the realities about parish stewardship, and what are the myths? What are the best practices in advancing parish stewardship?

In this chapter, we consider eight general stewardship strategies, along with their practical applications, that the data from our survey have shown to be most effective. Again, however, we must caution about reading too much into the direction of causality. Most of these strategies likely do lead to greater stewardship, but some might be the result of good stewardship that is already in place. The best we can really conclude is that they are associated with effective stewardship. At a minimum, we can conclude that these are the types of things that successful stewardship parishes do.

In selecting our eight strategies and the specific tactical activities within each, we focused on those activities that enhanced all four of our stewardship outcomes. In order to be truly a stewardship parish, a parish must do more than merely realize an increase in treasure, or more volunteer time, no matter how large those increases might be. Evidence of a true change of minds and hearts comes with increases in all three components of stewardship: time, talent, and treasure. Unless a parish has experienced increases in all three, it can't properly call itself a stewardship parish.

Best Practices in Parish Stewardship

The eight strategies are presented more or less in the order in which they should occur, although clearly there will be some overlap.

1) Be a welcoming parish that takes community-building seriously. People give to people. Unless a parish is viewed as a welcoming place, a place where there is a real sense of community — a place, as Justin Clements puts it, where people want to be — they are wasting their time talking about stewardship.

We found a few welcoming and community-building activities that were especially successful. Having greeters at Mass conveyed a welcoming atmosphere. Sponsoring functions like a parish picnic and potluck dinners gave parishioners from all segments of the parish community the opportunity to interact with those whom they might never otherwise have the opportunity to meet.

But the best course is to try a variety of approaches. The most successful stewardship parishes were those that sponsored four or more welcoming activities and those that sponsored four or more community-building events.

2) Appoint a stewardship council. Everyone who has studied stewardship has emphasized the importance of leadership. Successful parish stewardship begins at the top. But the pastor can't, and shouldn't, do it all by himself. He needs a competent stewardship council that will carry out the activities needed to create and maintain a sense of stewardship in the parish. We found that the specific organizational form that the stewardship council takes is less important than the characteristics of its members. Among other things, they should be spiritually motivated and living a life of stewardship. They need to have a vision of where stewardship can take the parish, be comfortable in talking about money, and recognize the importance of accountability.

3) **Include stewardship as a vital component of the parish plan.** One of the underlying themes of this book has been that to be successful, stewardship must permeate the entire parish. Every parish ministry needs to understand its role in advancing stewardship in the parish. To make this evident to everyone, a comprehensive discussion of the role of stewardship in the parish rightfully belongs in the parish plan, and specifically in the parish mission statement. Every action that the parish takes should be evaluated on how it fits into the parish plan for stewardship.

4) **Emphasize stewardship in all parish formation and education programs.** Keeping with the theme of the importance of stewardship permeating the entire parish, making stewardship an integral component of parish formation and education activities is essential. This is true for both youth and adult programs. Among the programs where a stewardship component had the greatest impact were religious education, youth groups, and nearly all adult education programs. But, as with so many of the strategies that we've reported on in this book, a combination of programs is most effective. Parishes that incorporated stewardship into three or more formation/education programs received significantly larger amounts of each of our stewardship outcomes.

5) **Provide the opportunity for lay witness presentations.** Lay witness presentations by parishioners — or, where appropriate, guest lay witnesses — can have a powerful effect on changing parishioners' minds and hearts. Listeners are motivated by hearing the lay witnesses' stories about their journeys and learning how stewardship affected their lives. Lay witness talks should occur more than once a year to emphasize that stewardship is not just about treasure.

Naturally, lay witnesses must be credible; their stewardship must have been intentional, and it must have encompassed all three components. Given those attributes, who should serve as a lay witness? It depends on the parish. Our data shows that it is important that the parish use at least some parishioners and not rely solely on guest lay witnesses. But aside from that, it depends on the demographic, socioeconomic, and cultural makeup of the parish as to what type of person would be most effective. Consistent with our findings for other stewardship strategies, we found support for using a variety of types of lay witnesses.

It doesn't seem to make a great deal of difference as to when the lay witness talk takes place (i.e., after the homily, after Communion, etc.), although lay witness talks at times other than Mass, while used by a small minority of parishes, were generally effective.

6) Encourage parishioners to make a commitment to the parish by pledging. Stewardship requires a commitment on the part of parishioners. That commitment could take the form of following the Biblical imperative to tithe one's income, but that is too narrow. It encompasses only one component of stewardship.

Pledging, though not a comfortable concept for most Catholics, can encompass all three stewardship components. In an earlier chapter, we discussed how pledging might be made more palatable to parishioners.

Whatever form the commitment takes, a stewardship parish needs to emphasize two facts to its parishioners: the importance of making a stewardship commitment to the parish, and the importance of that commitment reflecting the contribution of their first fruits.

7) Communicate with parishioners on stewardship. It is important for every parish to communicate with its parishioners. If we want them to take an active interest in the parish, we need to keep them informed on past and future activities. This is especially true for stewardship parishes. We need to communicate regularly with parishioners on both general stewardship topics and individual and group stewardship successes.

Parishes today have an assortment of media that they can use to communicate with parishioners. These include old standbys, such as announcements from the pulpit or information printed in the weekly bulletin. But these reach only those who are at Mass regularly. In this day and age, with fewer than a third of our parishioners at Mass on any given Sunday, it is imperative that we find communications media that can not only communicate with parishioners but also serve as evangelization tools.

One particularly successful communications medium is a newsletter sent to each parish household. Not only do newsletters reach those who weren't at Mass, but the format allows for a more in-depth presentation of issues, including those concerning stewardship. Although only a minority of parishes include stewardship information in their newsletters, it is an exceptionally effective means of increasing all four of our stewardship measures.

Another potentially effective medium for communicating on stewardship with parishioners is the parish Web site. We say potentially because, unfortunately, so few parishes use this method that we found its impact on stewardship outcomes to be limited. At the same time, we need to recognize the importance of technology in the lives of our young people. That is how they communicate. If we hope to reverse present trends and attract large numbers of our young adults back to full membership in the Church, we need to reach out to them by becoming more technologically sophisticated.

In any event, as with most of the other stewardship strategies that we analyzed, we found that communicating about stewardship through a variety of media was effective in increasing all four of our stewardship outcomes.

8) Remember that good stewardship starts in the parish house. This point is listed last only for emphasis; it actually should be first. If we want our parishioners to be good stewards of their resources, we need to model this behavior for them. The parish administration must be careful that its spending decisions reflect good stewardship, that it has in place effective internal financial controls, and that it is accountable and transparent in all its financial dealings. There are a number of venues for parishioners to carry out their stewardship. The parish is only one.

Parishioners won't contribute their time, talent, and treasure to an organization that is not prudent in its spending, serious about financial controls, or accountable and transparent in its finances.

We found that the most effective method for the parish to display its financial accountability and transparency is through regular budget reports included in the parish newsletter. On the other hand, the parish Web site is an ideal, if underutilized, method for achieving that same goal.

Summary

This book has attempted to cut through the anecdotal evidence and learn about the effectiveness of various parish stewardship activities. Along the way, we discovered some myths — stewardship practices that have a reputation for success, but are in fact either totally ineffective or only partially effective in advancing parish stewardship. We also discovered some realities — those stewardship activities that actually lived up to their reputation. These are the best practices.

Readers are urged to consider these findings and adapt them to their own parish situation. Only good things can come from parishes taking stewardship seriously.

Notes